SCHOOLS COUNCIL EXAMINATIONS BULLETIN 44

Hear/say:
a review of oral/aural
graded tests

DEREK UTLEY
ROSAMOND MITCHELL and
JEAN ANN PHILLIPS

prepared on behalf of the Coordinating
Committee for Graded Objectives in Modern
Languages

Methuen Educational

*First published 1983 for the Schools Council
Newcombe House, 45 Notting Hill Gate, London W11 3JB
by Methuen Educational
11 New Fetter Lane, London EC4P 4EE*

*Filmset in Monophoto Times
by Northumberland Press Ltd,
Gateshead
Printed in Great Britain by
Richard Clay (The Chaucer Press) Ltd
Bungay, Suffolk*

British Library Cataloguing in Publication Data
Utley, Derek
Hear/say—(*Schools Council examinations bulletins;* 44)
1. Grading and marking (*Students*)
I. Title   II. Mitchell, Rosamond
III. Phillips, Jean Ann   IV. Series
371.2′64   *LB3051*
ISBN 0–423–51250–1

Contents

Foreword

In 1980 the Schools Council embarked upon five programmes of work to be undertaken over three years. Programme 5 – Improving the Examinations System – covers a large number of activities related to examining, assessing and the recording of results.

The present review of current developments in modern languages' oral/aural graded tests was undertaken as part of this programme. The work was carried out on behalf of the Coordinating Committee for Graded Objectives in Modern Languages (GOML) as a result of a Programme 5 grant. Concurrent with this review the Council commissioned Andrew Harrison to undertake a broader investigation into graded tests in all subjects which resulted in the publication in 1982 of Schools Council Examinations Bulletin 41, *Review of Graded Tests*. In the previous year, the Council also published *Graded Objectives and Tests for Modern Languages: an Evaluation* by M. Buckby *et al.*, which examined the effects of graded tests on the attitudes of pupils, teachers and parents to the learning of French.

The special emphasis placed by the Schools Council on graded tests is due to its belief that they have recently had a significant effect on language testing and learning in Britain, and that they may well be of relevance for other subject areas in the future.

The present review was conducted by a GOML sub-committee, comprising Derek Utley, Rosamond Mitchell and Jean Ann Phillips, to whom the Council is grateful for a thorough investigation despite limited resources. Like all other Programme 5 projects, this project was overseen by the Programme's Monitoring and Review Group (a list of whose members is presented on p. 93).

GEOFF BARDELL
Principal Research Officer
Schools Council

Acknowledgements

This review owes much to many: to the groups who responded so fully to the questionnaire, to those who offered to write a commissioned report (whether or not the offer was taken up), and to those individuals and groups who put up with our correspondence, visits and interviews.

Andrew Harrison deserves our thanks for so willingly helping with the sending out of the questionnaires and processing of the statistical information in the returns, and his wife Mary for typing the reports so quickly and efficiently.

Geoff Bardell, of the Schools Council, provided firm yet unobtrusive support, and the GOML Coordinating Committee, from whom the idea for the report first sprang, gave useful guidance at crucial points.

The spirit of cooperation and involvement shown by virtually all those we approached made our task easy and pleasurable. It is also typical of so much that goes on in the graded objectives movement.

DEREK UTLEY

I. Introduction

Graded tests in modern languages have had a significant effect on the teaching and learning of modern languages in Britain since their emergence in the mid-1970s. The graded tests 'movement', which is in fact made up of a number of local independent groups, has devised tests at different levels, based on specific learning objectives. The popularity of these tests with teachers and learners is shown by the existence, in October 1982, of some 60 local groups offering tests for secondary school pupils across the ability range at up to five levels, mainly in French and German, but also in less widely taught languages such as Spanish and Italian. In 1979 the Coordinating Committee for Graded Objectives in Modern Languages (the GOML Coordinating Committee) was set up, partly funded by the Centre for Information on Language Teaching and Research (CILT), as a means to liaise and disseminate information between hitherto loosely connected groups. The *GOML Newsletter* (see Bibliography) has an important part to play in the spreading of news and ideas, and recently some research has been conducted into the effects and significance of graded tests and objectives, particularly in schools (Buckby *et al.*, 1981; Harrison, 1982; see Bibliography).

As part of this programme of research, in August 1980 the GOML Coordinating Committee applied to the Schools Council for a grant to enable it to administer a project to examine current work in the groups on the testing and teaching of oral and aural skills.

Project brief

The precise terms of the brief were to:

... examine current work in the groups on the assessment of defined objectives in oral/aural work in modern language learning, the methods used to achieve it, the problems encountered and the types of solution proposed. Proposals and recommendations for further work in modern languages and in other subject areas of the curriculum to which it was felt these findings might apply, would be made.

An interim and final report would be made to the Schools Council. It would be expected that the reports would include information about the interrelationship between graded objectives in teaching and testing programmes, the practicalities of test administration and the feasibility of large-scale application of these procedures. They would refer to criterion-referencing,* school-based assessment conducted by teachers, advantages and disadvantages of internal and external assessment, and the attainment of valid and reliable results.

The application was granted, and a subcommittee of the GOML Coordinating Committee was set up, consisting of:

> Jean Ann Phillips (Department of Education, University of Manchester)
> Rosamond Mitchell (Department of Education, University of Stirling)
> Derek Utley (York Language Training Limited)

Jean Ann Phillips acted as coordinator and conducted most of the interviews used as a basis for Chapter V, Rosamond Mitchell drafted Chapter IV, and Derek Utley compiled the report.

Significance of oral/aural skills

At a time when national criteria for a common system of examining at 16+ are being formulated with some urgency, any investigation into objectives and testing is bound to be relevant. The selection of oral/aural skills as a subject for special scrutiny was felt necessary for two main reasons:

> They are the two areas where most difficulty has been experienced in devising test forms based on communicative objectives; consequently, they show a sometimes bewildering diversity of approach.

> They have a significance for other subject areas which may be greater than is commonly believed, and which investigation may clarify.

For such a relatively modest report as this, it may seem overweening to provide a prescription for all areas of the curriculum. Our goal was in fact less ambitious, particularly as regards the implications for other subject areas, which are outlined in Chapter VI. It is worth noting here, however, that the implications are wide: from the reassessment of the pos-

---

* For a glossary of the more technical words used in this report see Appendix B.

sible role of the spoken word in our examination systems, through the kind of motivation likely to bring results, the setting of appropriate goals, the delicate question of scoring and assessing, to the kind of internal and external systems necessary to support, enrich and spread the teaching and testing of oral/aural skills.

Level of investigation

Our main concern was to gather information on 'what's going on out there', rather than 'what you think ought to be going on', and to produce a field report which would show the reality of the tests in action. As a result, much of the information contained here will be familiar to habitués of the movement. We hope, however, that it will offer information to the curious, new angles to the informed, and areas for further research and development to all.

Procedure

The work was carried out over a period of two years. Information was gathered by four main methods:

A questionnaire sent to all groups.

Commissioned reports (CRs): reports written by members of certain groups on subjects highlighted by returns to the questionnaire.*

Analysis of selected tests, in order to provide detailed information on the oral/aural content of a number of graded tests.

Recorded interviews. Members of certain groups were interviewed in order to give recent information and views on issues which had emerged as important in the development of oral/aural teaching and testing.

Further information on how this information-gathering was carried out will be found in relevant sections of the report.

---

* See Appendix A for details of the areas covered and the contributors' names.

II. The questionnaire

The subcommittee drafted a questionnaire to be sent to all groups, requesting information on their tests. The questions were grouped under the broad headings of development, availability, administration and assessment. To facilitate the work of the subcommittee and of the recipients, this questionnaire was included with the one being sent out by Andrew Harrison for the purpose of his review of graded tests (see Harrison, 1982). Questionnaires were returned from about seventy-five per cent of all groups (44 groups), and cover the three main languages French, German and Spanish.

Analysis of returns

Summaries of the questionnaire returns are presented in Tables 1–4, which give a more detailed question-by-question analysis.*

DEVELOPMENT (see Table 1)
Question 11.1† ('Who sets your tests?') gives a clear idea of members of a group working closely together. Perhaps more tests are derived from others than are shown here, but the emphasis is still on teamwork: individuals working together to respond to a range of specific local needs. Nowhere is an individual given as the developer of a set of tests.

Pre-testing (11.2: 'Do you undertake any pre-testing?') is carried out in about half the cases reported. Given the number of multiple-choice items used (see 13.8), more pre-testing might have been expected, but no doubt the practical implications of this have been a strong deterring factor. Where pre-testing *has* taken place, it is obvious that the most popular procedure is to pre-test the whole test (11.3: 'What is pre-tested?') and

---

*Questions 1–10 refer to the review of graded tests (published in Harrison, 1982), and are analysed there.

†The numbers in parentheses in the remainder of this section refer to particular questions in the questionnaire.

Table 1 The development of oral (O)/aural(A) tests

Question	French		German		Spanish		Total	
	O	A	O	A	O	A	O	A
11.1 Tests set by teachers	8	8	3	3	2	2	13	13
work group	13	13	12	12	8	8	33	33
OMLAC* group	2	2	2	2	0	0	4	4
miscellaneous	7	7	1	3	0	0	8	10
11.2 Pre-testing? Yes	15	15	11	12	8	8	34	35
No	21	21	9	8	3	3	33	32
11.3 Pre-testing of individual items	1	1	0	0	0	0	1	1
of sections	1	2	0	1	0	0	1	3
of full test	12	12	10	11	7	8	29	31
11.4 Size of pre-test population	— between 100 and 2000 —							
11.5 Selection of pre-test population	— usually ad hoc —							

* Oxford Modern Language Achievement Certificate.

not just the multiple-choice component, which is more susceptible to, and in need of, statistical analysis. The size (11.4) and method of selection (11.5) of the pre-test population obviously depend heavily on local conditions, and no pattern of procedure emerges from the returns.

AVAILABILITY (see Table 2)

There appeared to be a strong feeling that the tests should be available on demand, and this is in fact the case in the majority of groups (12.1: 'When are the tests available?'), although there is probably some overlap between 'on demand' and 'within a period'. Where the tests have already been written and put into operation they can be made available when considered appropriate. Where tests are in the process of preparation (at Levels 3 and 4 for example), availability may be restricted by the time-table of the composers. The issue of availability is closely linked with the question of flexibility of progress of individuals or groups through the system; the more limited is the availability, the more likely a teacher is to be tied to a 'lock-step' style of progress.

Preparation for the tests (12.2: 'How do candidates prepare for the tests?') is usually ensured by familiarizing learners with the kind of material to be used, or by general preparation, presumably along very similar lines. An interesting feature here is the number of cases (13 overall) in which pupils actually saw or heard the materials to be used. It is not clear how specific these materials are – whether they are defined in precise

Table 2   The availability of oral(O)/aural(A) tests

Question	French		German		Spanish		Total	
	O	A	O	A	O	A	O	A
12.1 Available on demand	20	19	13	12	5	4	38	35
within a period	11	11	6	7	5	6	22	24
at other times	2	2	0	0	1	1	3	3
12.2 Candidates prepare by:								
knowing actual material	7	0	4	0	2	0	13	0
knowing kind of material	22	25	11	12	7	8	40	45
general preparation	16	12	11	12	4	4	31	28
12.3 Confidentiality a problem?								
Yes	0	0	0	0	0	0	0	0
No	31	31	18	18	9	10	58	59
12.4 Will it be a problem in any public examination?								
Yes	4	4	3	3	2	2	9	9
No	12	11	8	7	3	2	23	20
Not applicable	18	18	8	8	5	5	31	31

lexical terms, or whether they are on a global or merely functional level, for example – but the idea of 'leaking' all or some of the components of a test has great methodological interest. It will also raise a few eyebrows in more conventional examining circles. Reference is made to this practice in Commissioned Report IV (CR IV).

In view of the above, it is no surprise that confidentiality is never considered a problem (12.3). Even when contact with public examinations hoves into view (12.4: 'Do you see confidentiality becoming a problem if you are adapting your scheme for public examinations?') – and it does so only in about half the cases shown – the majority of respondents do not see confidentiality as a major problem. It is not clear why this is. Will the same openness carry through? Will groups conform strictly to examination boards' procedure? Will the tests be completely rewritten each year? Or is it because teachers already consider themselves experienced in Mode III examination practice, with which the graded tests will have a lot in common? An even more positive view might be that a truly communicative test would give credit for spontaneity, and play down the value of rote learning, especially if inappropriately applied.

ADMINISTRATION (see Table 3)

Although question 13 shows that the vast majority of tests are administered by the class teacher, there is a significant number of cases where other teachers or 'outsiders' are brought in (13.1: 'Who administers the test?'). The use of advisers, assistants and college students suggests an attempt to break away from the confines of the teacher-pupil classroom situation towards a more realistic form of communication.

Briefing is carried out by all groups (13.2: 'What briefing does the tester receive about test administration?'). Just about every oral/aural (O/A) test has written documentation available, and the closeness of relationships within the group is again shown by the heavy incidence of meetings and informal consultations. The one mention of in-service education and training (INSET) is the only explicit reference to what, given the innovative and collaborative nature of the tests, must be a recurrent feature.

The timing of the administration of the tests (13.3: 'When are the tests administered?') suggests a wide variety of approaches to a real problem. The majority of tests are set in normal class time, and examination periods offer a useful opportunity for fitting tests in. But there is a very strong suggestion of teachers giving up their own lunchtimes and after-school time. Not stated, but clearly to be deduced from this, are two facts: first, that teachers feel it is worthwhile to give up this time and, second, that pupils also are motivated enough to give up their own free time to take part in the tests.

From questions 13.4 ('How many candidates are tested simultaneously?') and 13.5 ('How long do the tests take?') it can be seen that usually the oral test is given to pupils one at a time, and takes just under five minutes, whilst typically the aural test is given to the whole class, and takes about thirty minutes. Exceptions to this norm are usually the use of pair or group assessment, in which both skills are assessed together on the basis of a short period of pupil interaction assessed by the teacher.

The tape recorder is the equipment most used in the two kinds of test (13.6: 'What equipment is used for testing, other than test sheets?'). In the aural test, however, a large number prefer to do without it, presumably choosing to have the language read out by the teacher. This raises the issues of validity, fairness and authenticity, issues taken up in the commissioned reports. Another, similar, issue is whether to tape the candidate's oral performance; the indication here is that only in 16 of the tests is the tape recorder used, even though in question 13.9 it is claimed that the candidates are recorded in 37 cases! An encouraging number of

Table 3   The administration of oral (O)/aural (A) tests

Question	French O	French A	German O	German A	Spanish O	Spanish A	Total O	Total A
13.1 Administered by:								
class teacher	34	34	20	20	11	11	65	65
other teacher	3	2	4	3	2	2	9	7
assistant	7	6	3	3	2	2	12	11
senior pupil	1	1	0	0	0	0	1	1
peer pupil	0	0	0	0	0	0	0	0
visitors	1	1	1	1	0	0	2	2
advisory staff	1	0	1	0	1	0	3	0
college students	1	1	0	0	0	0	1	1
13.2 Briefing:								
none	0	0	0	0	0	0	0	0
meetings	22	22	12	12	7	7	41	41
written documentation	30	30	15	15	11	11	56	56
informal consultation	13	13	8	8	3	3	24	24
INSET	1	1	0	0	0	0	1	1
13.3 When administered?								
Timetabled class time	30	31	17	18	10	10	57	59
Other school time	20	8	16	7	9	4	45	19
School exams	15	18	9	11	6	8	30	37
Outside school time	8	1	7	1	3	0	18	2
13.4 Number of candidates tested simultaneously:								
whole class	1	31	1	19	0	11	2	61
group	3	5	4	2	2	2	9	9
pair	5	1	2	0	2	0	9	1
individual	33	3	17	2	10	0	60	5
13.5 Length of test								
0–2 minutes ⎫	1	—	1	—	0	—	2	—
3–5 minutes ⎪ oral	26	—	10	—	8	—	44	—
6–10 minutes ⎬	2	—	2	—	1	—	5	—
10+ minutes ⎭	1	—	0	—	0	—	1	—
0–5 minutes ⎫	—	1	—	0	—	0	—	1
6–15 minutes ⎪	—	3	—	1	—	1	—	5
16–25 minutes ⎬ aural	—	20	—	12	—	6	—	38
26–35 minutes ⎪	—	6	—	4	—	2	—	12
36–45 minutes ⎪	—	3	—	1	—	1	—	5
46–60 minutes ⎭	—	1	—	1	—	0	—	2

Table 3 *cont.*

Question	French		German		Spanish		Total	
	O	*A*	*O*	*A*	*O*	*A*	*O*	*A*
13.6 Equipment used:								
none	17	14	8	8	6	5	31	27
tape recorder	10	18	4	13	2	5	16	36
language laboratory	3	3	0	0	1	0	4	3
visuals	10	3	7	2	4	0	21	5
realia	7	1	5	0	2	1	14	2
overhead projector	2	2	1	1	0	0	3	3
13.7 Advice on prompting:								
discretion	13	—	10	—	5	—	28	—
prescribed lines	17	—	7	—	5	—	29	—
not permitted	5	—	3	—	1	—	9	—
none given	1	—	0	—	0	—	1	—
13.8 Form of response:								
multi-choice pictures	—	4	—	2	—	1	—	7
multi-choice in foreign language	—	10	—	5	—	3	—	18
multi-choice in English	—	28	—	19	—	10	—	57
written in foreign language	—	3	—	1	—	1	—	5
written in English	—	18	—	10	—	5	—	33
13.9 Candidate recorded?								
Yes	22	—	11	—	4	—	37	—
No	15	—	9	—	7	—	31	—
13.10 How many?								
All	13	—	7	—	3	—	23	—
Sample	10	—	5	—	1	—	16	—

oral tests (and some aural) use visuals and realia, and at least some language laboratories are still alive and well; the relative newcomer, the overhead project (OHP), is already apparent if not widespread. Prompting in the oral test (13.7: 'What advice is given to testers on prompting?') is as often left to the discretion of the tester as it is prescribed. In a few cases it is not allowed – presumably where the need for objectivity overrides the desire for naturalism – but only very rarely is the question of prompting ignored.

The most popular form of response in the aural test (13.8: 'What form do candidates' responses take?') is multiple-choice in English, though a significant number used written answers in English (presumably, either objective or open-ended), and there was also support for multiple-choice in the foreign language. A few used multiple-choice pictures, whilst there were five cases of written answers in the foreign language. Behind this surprisingly wide range of approaches can be detected a certain amount of polemic (or healthy disagreement?) which in turn reflects attitudes towards 'realistic' situations, the separation or mixing of skills and the relative importance of objectivity – issues which are taken up later.

Apparently, more candidates have their oral performance recorded than not (13.9: 'Are candidates' test performances recorded?'), but the difference (37 as against 31) is not as great as might have been imagined, given the needs of moderation, or even initial assessment. Considerations of time and practicality will no doubt carry weight in this decision, but it is interesting to see (13.10: 'If yes, how many?') that in the majority of cases, once the tape recorder is in use, all pupils are recorded rather than a sample. This suggests the recording may be used for subsequent assessment, and not only for moderation purposes (see also question 14.3 on the scoring of the tests).

ASSESSMENT (see Table 4)
The mechanics of scoring the tests, and pre-test briefing, follow the pattern of test administration. They are usually scored by the class teacher (14.1: 'Who scores the tests?'), sometimes by other teachers, and occasionally by 'outsiders' (see 13.1). Written documentation is again the most common means of briefing (14.2: 'What briefing does the person scoring the tests receive?'), followed by meetings, both before and after the test, and informal consultation. The 'note to the aberrant scorer' may or may not go with an adjustment of marks to keep them in line, and is presumably aimed at improving next year's performance. This procedure is perhaps a simple form of in-service education and training.

Table 4   The assessment of oral (O)/aural (A) tests

Question	French O	French A	German O	German A	Spanish O	Spanish A	Total O	Total A
14.1 Tests scored by:								
class teacher	34	34	20	20	11	11	65	65
other teacher	6	6	3	3	2	2	11	11
assistant	3	1	3	2	2	1	8	4
visitors	1	1	1	1	0	0	2	2
14.2 Briefing of scorer:								
pre-test meeting(s)	21	21	10	10	6	5	37	36
post-test meeting(s)	9	8	3	1	3	2	15	11
written documentation	32	31	16	14	11	10	59	55
informal consultation	13	13	7	7	3	3	23	23
'note to aberrant scorer'	1	0	1	0	0	0	2	0
INSET	1	1	0	0	0	0	1	1
14.3 When scored?								
During test	27	—	16	—	8	—	51	—
Subsequently	4	—	2	—	1	—	7	—
Either	5	—	3	—	2	—	10	—
14.4 System of assessment:								
individual utterances	24	—	14	—	9	—	47	—
global/overall	2	—	2	—	2	—	6	—
overall, on specified range	2	—	2	—	2	—	6	—
mixed system	10	—	5	—	1	—	16	—
14.5 Adjustment of marks?								
Yes	14	8	9	4	5	3	28	15
No	23	27	11	13	6	7	40	47
14.6 Continuous assessment?								
Yes	8	6	5	2	3	1	16	9
No	26	29	14	17	7	9	47	55
Of what form? – various!	9	8	5	4	3	3	17	15

The large majority of oral tests are scored during the test (14.3: 'When are the tests scored?'), with scoring being left until afterwards only in seven cases. This is surprising, in view of the large number who use the tape recorder. Interestingly, in ten instances a choice is allowed – presumably another example of individual autonomy within a group.

The question on the system of assessment used (14.4: 'On what system is candidates' oral performance assessed?') showed that there was an overwhelming preference for marking individual utterances. This type of marking is suited to language which is divided into a number of short statements, that is, role-play, or responses to separate questions. The relative shortage of global-type assessment, with or without a specified range, suggests that 'free' conversation is either restricted because so many of the tests still only cover the first few levels, or is elicited in such a way as to take the shape of a number of short utterances, even at the higher levels. There is also a strong possibility that in the 16 instances where a 'mixed system' is used, role-play is assessed on the basis of individual utterances, and conversation on a global system.

The internal, immediate nature of the tests and their certification is brought out by the response to the question on adjustment (14.5: 'Do any procedures exist for adjusting the marks after the test has been scored?'), which suggests that the initial assessment, however reached, stands without being subject to moderation in the majority of cases. It cannot be seen from the table how this situation varies with the level reached, but there is no doubt that contact with public examinations will make some form of external moderation increasingly necessary. Continuous assessment is a relatively new development in modern language learning, and it is one that the graded test movement has brought to the fore. It is not surprising, therefore, to see that about one-quarter of the responses to question 14.6 ('Is there any element of continuous assessment?') are positive in the case of the oral test, and about one-seventh in the aural test. Continuous assessment may take a variety of forms, from subjective teacher assessment, through a series of mini- or 'waystage' tests, to pupils' progress cards or checklists combined with paired pupil interaction monitored by a teacher/assessor. The latter types, in particular, represent more than a slight refinement in testing techniques; embodied in them are a number of assumptions and attitudes which extend well into the organization of teaching itself. These will be discussed later.

General features of the returns

In addition to the factual information yielded by the analysis of the returns, and summarized above, the questionnaire pointed clearly to a number of areas for further investigation by means of the commissioned reports. There also emerged a number of general features which are worth listing here:

Balance. Within each group, the statistics for the oral and aural tests are more similar than might be expected. There is little difference, for example, between the figures for the two skills in the areas of pre-testing and briefing. There is also a very close similarity in the way in which the three languages (French, German and Spanish) are treated – not surprisingly, given the involvement of the same teachers. The lack of balance in the numbers involved in the different languages is similarly predictable, given the customary predominance of French, especially in the early, non-selective area of language learning, at which many of the graded tests are aimed; however, it should not, for that reason, be allowed to pass without comment or regret. Many a trail has been blazed through the jungle by French-teaching pioneers; their German and Spanish counterparts should find the going that much easier, and the opportunity for further refinement and improvement should not be neglected.

The Jekyll and Hyde syndrome. Attitudes to decision-making and problem-solving revealed by comments on the questionnaires range between two poles: a tentative, doubting attitude which recognizes the complexities of many of the issues involved and the lack of experience in the movement to solve them; and the swashbuckling, confident approach which emphasizes the enormous breakthrough and consolidation carried out so far, with the conviction that momentum and expertise will carry the movement through any future obstacles. References to 'inadequacy', 'lack of experience' and 'problem area' are as common as are references to successes scored and the ability to 'grow with the new challenge'. No one person or group necessarily embodies both these attitudes, or even any single one of them, but both exist closely together, and are based in a very firm if ambivalent reality … without, of course, any of the sinister implications of the original Mr Hyde.

Teamwork. Much of the experience and expertise in oral/aural tests is embodied in individuals or groups, each with their own specialization in such areas as continuous assessment, unit credits, communication theory or assessment of communicative performance. But more striking than a cast list is the impression conveyed of a joint effort in which experience is shared both within and between the groups, and this is true despite (because of?) an unprecedented degree of autonomy between individuals and groups. It is one of the characteristics whose implications cannot be over-stressed, and which reappeared in the commissioned reports.

Questions arising from the analysis

After an initial study of the questionnaire returns, a list of areas was drawn up which were known to be crucial to the development of oral/ aural graded tests, and a number which were new enough to be relatively undocumented. Colleagues active in these areas were asked to write a report giving more details. The main areas which were followed up are outlined below.

The definition of separate skills. The assumption that oral and aural skills could be separated in practice was challenged more than once. More information was required on the desirability and practicability of testing them separately or together.

Practical considerations. These were widespread, and often of paramount concern to the groups. They ranged from the logistical problems of a group covering a wide geographical area, to the question of how to fit 30 oral tests into a 35-minute lesson. This spectrum could be exemplified in any one of a multitude of ways: it would not be untypical to envisage a German teacher trying to find a colleague to take a netball practice, in order to travel 30 miles (at the teacher's own expense) to attend a 5 p.m. meeting at which to contribute views on possible exponents of a functional syllabus, based on a French original discussed at the previous meeting, and report on the availability of a German friend to record any listening tests, should it be decided to record them. This vision is simplistic rather than grotesque, as will be seen from subsequent analysis; the only accurate general statement that can be made is that each group endeavours to find its own solution.

Test type and content. The actual form and administering of the tests themselves were dependent on a wide range of other factors, from communication theory, through syllabus design, to practical constraints of the kind mentioned above. Some groups construct tests purely intuitively, from a sense of what is right, but the suitability of their form and content requires input from linguists, practising school teachers and those with an administrative function.

Cueing. If the tests are to be more than a string of spoken or written questions, and if they are to recreate some kind of communicative reality, the range of materials and techniques available for cueing will need to be reappraised thoroughly and imaginatively.

Assessment strategies. We needed to know more about how tests were marked (globally, discreetly, with specified criteria or subjectively); how they were moderated, if at all; how the oral/aural component was represented on the certificate; and what were the relative merits of continuous and summative assessment.

Evaluation. After assessment comes test evaluation. We would need to know whether groups were evaluating the tests and their effects on pupils and teachers, and if they were reviewing the validity of the tests by checking them against the syllabus.

III. Views from the groups

We attempted via the commissioned reports to gather information on all the points mentioned at the end of the last chapter. The information and opinions gathered from the nine reports commissioned have been combined in this section, arranged under headings which reflect the most recurrent themes. Facts and theories, triumphs and concerns thus combine to give a picture of the state of the art in oral/aural graded tests, and point the way to future developments.*

Matching the pressures

Involvement in oral/aural graded tests requires a wide range of skills and activities, and exerts great pressures on teachers. Some of these pressures are very specific, others are more pervasive yet less tangible. It is worth stating this latter category first, to show the backdrop against which decisions have to be taken.

Variety or standardization? The common problems posed to groups by the need to set a large number of original tests have been met in a correspondingly large number of ways. This wide variety of responses to both central and peripheral issues, depending on local requirements and strengths, is a reflection of healthy local autonomy. It is a strength of the movement, which groups in other curriculum areas may wish to bear in mind. It is also a divisive influence, which spreads effort unnecessarily and deprives the movement of the common voice which will become increasingly necessary as contact with the public examination boards increases.

Intimacy or popularity? Continuous growth also affects the nature of individual groups. In some areas, a small group of enthusiasts has expanded into a large body which cannot hope to have the same flexibility or sense of pioneering. Success is thus a major and irresistible instrument

* A list of the titles and authors of the reports is in Appendix A. The numbers used (such as C R V) refer to the numbers given to each report in the Appendix.

of change; recognition of this phenomenon is a necessary first stage in adapting structures and attitudes to the new and still-changing situation. The effect of growth can also be seen below, under 'Practicalities'.

The ideal or the possible? Many of the groups are aware that their tests are evolving rapidly, along with syllabuses and teaching methods. Consequently, many questions remain to be resolved before the 'ideal' situation can be agreed upon, let alone put into practice; there is a wide span between writing a paper on communication theory and getting a test certificate handed out. Instead of waiting for the ideal solution, however, groups are getting on with running the tests, warts and all, in the knowledge that they are, at least, a vast improvement on what went before, in terms of pupils' achievement and motivation.

Certificates or education? For the pupil the test certificate is a goal and a visible sign of achievement, and so a great motivator. In the early days, and particularly for weaker pupils, it may also have been the basis for an almost complete teaching programme. Time and experience have made for a change in emphasis, in which priority is given to good teaching practice, and to devising a test which will reflect it. Attitudes to testing are, therefore, increasingly concerned with listening and speaking as acts of communication, and with the classroom and testing situations which best reflect real communication. As such, the graded oral/aural tests and the activities leading up to them are seen as a truly educative process. No doubt the teacher will welcome both the piece of paper and the educational philosophy – but the two will take some reconciling.

Practicalities

Many of the practical problems which accompany the oral/aural tests will be proportionate to the size of the group in terms of numbers of members and geographical area. One of the largest groups – in both respects – is the Cumbria/Lancashire group, on which many of the observations made here are based. In this, as in other groups, the commitment to decentralization and teacher involvement is clear. However involved the process of testing may appear, from conception to post-test evaluation, it is as well to remember that it is further complicated by the fact that it takes place (or much of it takes place) not in a vacuum, but in a school environment itself rich in intricacy, if not frustration. Classroom teachers will need no reminding.

Re-cycling. The prodigious effort required to get group members to devise, produce, administer and assess just one level of tests should not hide the fact that in the following year the same tests, with any necessary improvements, will need to be re-cycled at the same time as the next level is being developed. This need to keep many balls in the air at the same time will be a feature of the first four or five years of a group's existence (most groups are still well within this period – see Harrison, 1982, Appendix A, Table 1), after which the problems of variety of activity will come to be replaced by those of ever-increasing size and of revision and development. In Cumbria/Lancashire, for example, during the course of 1981/2, French Levels 1 and 2, German Level 1 and Spanish Level 1 were made available (to about 30 000 candidates), whilst German Level 2 and Spanish Level 2 were in their second year of pre-testing. Variety of activity may make life more interesting, but it is a factor which will put a strain on teachers and resources.

Availability. Linked to the above point is the question of availability of tests. Once developed, in order to make teaching and testing programmes as flexible and learner-orientated as possible, they should be available at any time – a requirement which is ideally filled by continuous assessment.

Continuous assessment also allows for a degree of flexibility in the timing of the tests; for example, problems of absentees are easily solved. (C R V)

It should be noted, however, that such assessment requires a continuous administrative process.

The flying teacher. The devising and assessing of suitable oral/aural tests – which may include a variety of non-verbal stimuli or other carefully thought-out attempts to recreate a genuinely communicative situation, texts of a suitable standard and multiple-choice answers – requires not just time, but discussion. Given the nature of some of the groups, this means travel as well as the inevitable meetings. Faced with this problem to a greater degree than most, Cumbria/Lancashire have come up with two complementary solutions: area working groups, and a more radical five-day residential meeting. The benefits of the latter are clearly spelled out:

By the arranging of a five-day meeting in a residential centre, considerable savings were made on travelling expenses and, given that all the teachers were absent from their schools for a period of more than three days, it was possible for their schools to bring in supply teachers to cover their work. In addition, removed for a period from their day-to-day school responsibilities, the teachers were able to apply themselves fully to the task in hand, giving it their undivided attention and making what could have been a protracted and boring process into an enjoyable and stimulating process. (C R II)

These benefits should be recognized (by local education authorities (L E As), for example) as a clear incentive to organize large groups along the lines of decentralized area meetings and larger, intensive residential meetings.

Premises. Ideas are best pooled and arrangements best made in a convivial setting. The importance of the availability of teachers' centres, colleges and universities to the graded test movement should not be underestimated.

People. Premises do not let themselves. They are made available by people. The role of 'leaders' or coordinators from the kinds of establishment mentioned above has been crucial to the graded test movement, and will need to be noted by other subject areas thinking of following a similar line of development. The tests appear to be 'free', or nearly so; but expense should be viewed in terms of human resources as well as financial.

Communications. One expense which will increase with the size of the group is postage and telephone costs. These may well be lost in the overheads of a sponsoring L E A or other body, but they are an example of the kind of issue which may well need to be explicitly resolved as graded tests become more widespread. The resourcefulness with which Cumbria/Lancashire have tackled the problem – via internal mail, meetings and teaching practice visits – is noteworthy.

Pre-test or cross your fingers? Many groups are interested in using multiple-choice answers in the aural test; many already use them (see 'Analysis of returns', question 13.8). To be reliable, they should be pre-tested, but this takes time and resources. The dilemma is stated in C R VII.

We would like to be able to do this [the pre-testing of our test materials and the analysis of the results] efficiently, thoroughly and effectively. We are a working group of full-time teachers. We hold all our meetings and do all our work outside normal working hours. Readily available guidelines, some kind of a framework and help with the analysis of the results would be time-saving and valuable.

At the moment, half of the tests appear to be pre-tested (there is no indication of how thoroughly), and half appear to rely on the intuition of teachers as to how they performed.

Finding the time. Having sorted out all the problems of setting and producing the test, the teacher – and/or allies – has to administer it. The attempted streamlining of this process is one of the features of oral/aural tests; the oral, for example, takes less than five minutes per pupil in the majority of cases. But there is no perfectly easy solution: either the teacher's private time (already severely restricted) or precious teaching time must be given up, with consequent physical and mental fatigue. Again, the results must repay all the effort, but there are two pointers towards a greater rationalization: first, the development of a simpler and less onerous form of assessment, using a continuous process of pair assessment; and second, the expectation (implicit rather than explicit in the reports) that, as the tests become more widely accepted and more familiar, they will find a regular place in the structure of school time.

Evaluation. Although some groups talk about the improvement of their tests in the light of experience, there is little, if any, mention of the methods used. Perhaps the limited time available is better spent on more pressing things; perhaps teacher experience and intuition are good enough as tools for evaluation. But there will probably come a time when it will not be sufficient to adopt what may be the current approach of simply sitting down and asking: 'What do you think about that, then?'

Content

Behind the search for realistic and practicable objectives and tests which characterizes the graded test movement, lies a key principle which needs to be made explicit here: needs analysis. Instead of bringing down the tablets of stone, structurally/grammatically inscribed, and dumping them on the heads of the waiting (or, more usually, distracted) multitude, Moses has taken to scrutinizing his tribe, perhaps conducting a poll, and to editing the message heavily. Both the scrutiny and the editing are still in their relative infancy, but the fact that they take place means that the message is no longer sacred nor immutable. This is clear from all the commissioned reports, particularly I, IV and VI.

Syllabus design and language description. The oral/aural tests all have in common the assumption that they are based on a series of language tasks. The definition of these tasks, or of their types, is less uniform. They can be based exclusively on topics (such as 'hobbies', 'school') and situations ('shopping', 'way-finding'), on more or less detailed lists of functions and notions, on 'areas of communication' which span broad activities such as 'expressing opinions' or 'obtaining services', on language points, grammar or lexis. The most typical approach is a mixture of all of the above (see Chapter IV, 'Syllabus'). Such an eclectic attitude probably reflects the developing state of the art of language description, as well as the catholic dynamism of the groups. The lack of a common view of language, or of a common order of priorities (the importance of transferability, predictability and affective language, for example) could, however, prove an obstacle to the cross-fertilization of ideas between the groups.

The definition of separate skills. The subcommittee had already had some doubts as to whether the oral and aural skills could realistically be considered separately, and C R IV was commissioned with this specifically in mind (see 'The definition of separate skills', p. 22). Although certain forms of listening (e.g. to the radio) can be considered discrete, it is difficult to conceive of a conversation (the form taken by most oral tests) in which listening does not play a crucial part. Is it reasonable or realistic to assess just the one part of a conversation (speaking), simply because the other part (listening) might lend itself more conveniently to another form of test, itself quite discrete?

At these levels (3 and 4) there is less predictability of response to an utterance. Also, students must be in a position to respond intelligently to speech acts on the part of the native-speakers. Inevitably these tests are less prescribed, to allow development and creativity. (C R I V)

If the answer is 'no', then the tester must face the difficult task of finding the means to assess the two skills at the same time, a task made even more necessary at higher levels, where the requirements of realism make separation increasingly undesirable.

It is only at more sophisticated levels of interaction that prediction of response becomes difficult and separation of speaking from listening becomes less possible and – if we respect potential naturalistic settings – less desirable in testing techniques. (C R I V)

Much remains to be discussed and decided on the form and the assessment of an aural component in an oral test.

Did authenticity necessarily imply mixed-skill testing? Should there be an 'aural response' to an oral situation, e.g. by writing down received information? ... We decided not to pursue mixed-skill testing. This was a conscious decision, taken after much experimentation and discussion. We felt that for the pupil it was confusing under test conditions; for the total mark-scheme it was less straightforward; and it could only arise naturally in a restricted number of situations. (C R VII)

Weighting v. reliability. Speaking is the most interactive of the language skills, and probably the most useful, so it is not surprising that many of the reports mention its often ludicrous weighting in most present public examinations:

'Enlightened' teachers frequently feel guilty as they encourage sixth formers to engage in interesting group oral work, transcription, monitoring etc., in the knowledge that the nearest the student will get to being assessed on such is an unexpectedly difficult or a predictably boring oral (worth 10%) and/or an unnatural listening exercise set in multi-choice because it suits the Examining Board to mark it by computer. (CR IX)

and the need to correct this.

... the steering group have stressed from the outset that *use* of the target language, albeit at a modest communicative level in the early stages, must be accorded a correspondingly important place both in the conduct of the Level 1 test and in the actual weighting given it within the overall marking scheme.... We allocated 35 marks to the Speaking Test i.e. a weighting of 46·6%. This figure caused a few raised eyebrows at a CILT meeting but we were equally dismayed by the seemingly lesser importance accorded to the oral by schemes elsewhere in the country. (CR III)

The reports also point out that two great stumbling blocks to a more realistic weighting are the time necessary to test speaking adequately, and the dangers of the unreliability of subjective assessment.

All the perennial problems of the disproportionate time involved – between 4 and 10 minutes per pupil depending on their ability, the teacher's desire for utter fairness, the satisfactory or unsatisfactory nature of the conditions for testing – for what is a small proportion of the total mark, have bedevilled us. (CR VIII)

To a lesser degree, the same points could be made about the skill of listening.

The role of the tape-recorder. A tape-recorder may be used to present the material of the listening test, and it may be used to record the speaking test. These are two quite distinct uses, and there is disagreement – or difference of practice – in both cases. The question of whether the listening test should be taped is well presented by the member of a group which decided to use the teacher's voice instead of a tape-recorder:

Much discussion was devoted to whether or not the test should be taped, and copies sent to schools. After a great deal of discussion such a course was decided against, partly on educational grounds, partly for reasons of expediency. Although it was argued that to tape the question paper would ensure that every pupil heard the questions read at a uniform speed, and in a 'neutral' voice, there were, in our opinion, stronger reasons against it:

1 The cost, both in terms of cassettes and time of doing the actual recording.
2 Allied to (1), the difficulty of obtaining really professional recording conditions to produce a whole range of tapes ...
3 The difficulty of ensuring that every school possessed, and could operate effectively, sound equipment of sufficient quality that every candidate could hear absolutely clearly ...

4 Although uniformity and neutrality were fine in theory, in practice there was a lot to be said for a class being able to listen to the voice of the teacher they know and whose voice they were familiar with.

The need to repeat certain sections of each paper also made it administratively easier with 'live' performance rather than recorded input. (CR VIII)

The question of whether to record the speaking test was rarely exposed; as recordings are usually made for the purpose of marking and/or moderation, it is more suitable to consider this question under the heading of assessment.

Narrative context. Some groups present the listening and reading tests together in a narrative context. This is done as a matter of policy, and in the interests of realism.

In any 'real' situation of using or encountering language one does not pick a person up and drop him into a situation which has neither introduction nor consequence. It seemed to us that one of the problems facing many learners in tests was that of trying to grapple with a whole set of discrete items, each apparently complete in themselves, and with no relationship to anything that had gone before or was to occur after it. In life we are not picked up, dropped into the middle of a situation, asked to cope with it, and then wafted in some mysterious manner to the next, totally unrelated situation. (CR VIII)

Other groups either ignore this practice, or are unaware of it, and present a string of unrelated items in the listening (and the reading) test.

Multiple-choice or ... Multiple-choice options as answers to the questions in the aural test have three distinct advantages: they are easy to mark, their marking is objective and reliable, and they allow discrete sampling of the syllabus. They have equally distinct drawbacks: they are time-consuming to construct, they should really be subjected to an equally time-consuming shredding and pre-testing process; it has been claimed that they are by their very nature norm-referenced; and they present an unrealistic and non-communicative language task. It might also be argued that their composition is an extremely subjective process, not necessarily redeemed by pre-testing, and that the discrete form of test that they often lead to will have a very 'bitty' non-communicative appearance. This latter criticism will be forestalled, in part at least, by the kind of narrative technique referred to above. It would be wrong to suggest that the groups have not weighed up these arguments in reaching their decision to use foreign language or English multiple-choice answers, but the issues need to be clearly re-stated; expediency and success were, again, no doubt important considerations. There is a possibility, however, that multiple-choice techniques – at one time a 'breakthrough' – have simply been in-herited, and have not been subjected to the close scrutiny required by a thorough analysis of needs and communicative realism. Such rigour, of course, will have to be applied to any possible alternatives.

... open-ended questions. These are the most likely type of alternative within an aural test. Given that understanding of a spoken text has to be shown in some manner, the main possibilities will be translation (never mentioned in the questionnaire or reports), summary, or questions. The main problem with open-ended questions in English (surprisingly, a small number of tests use the mixed – and difficult – skill of written questions in the foreign language) is the subjective element of the marking process. With one-word answers, which some groups favour, especially at the lower levels, there is less difficulty than with the more lengthy and complex language required later on. But this is essentially a teacher/assessor problem, whose solution appears not too difficult, given the amount of experience gained in, for example, current CSE and GCE practice. Another possible objection, which may sometimes be overlooked, is the question of understanding on the part of the pupil. A commissioned report clearly makes the point that many of the limitations we have become aware of, particularly in the area of literacy, apply to performance in English as well as in the foreign language.

The pupils which Level 1 is now hoping to encompass (hitherto outside the scope of existing public examinations) are in the bottom 25 per cent of the ability range. They have specific problems which are identifiable in reading and writing skills in English and it may reasonably be assumed that the same weaknesses in literacy will be evident in the foreign language, not to say compounded by being in a language which is not their mother tongue. (CR VI)

It is important to show that the comprehension we are testing is that of the foreign language text.

Cueing a response. The same problem will arise, in a slightly different guise, in the question of the cueing of the tasks in the oral test. The over-all form and flavour of an oral test will depend on two major areas of teacher input: the setting and the type of stimulus on the one hand, and the criteria adopted for assessing the response on the other. Decisions can be made on the basis of intuition or expediency, but these will still reflect an idea of what communication is or should be; the constraints of the classroom testing situation will be apparent, but should not be over-riding. One of the commissioned reports has many useful observations on the best means of re-creating a communicative reality within a test situation, as well as in a teaching programme.

Tests of communicative ability are not necessarily confined to one or even two of the skills. For instance in taking account of the potential communicative needs of the learner it is possible to conceive of authentic communicative tasks such as:

a [classroom activity] read adverts for penpals in a foreign teenage magazine, discuss them with your partner in order to choose a suitable penpal each and write off to the addresses given in the advert or ...

b [real-life/simulation] read the advertisement for a restaurant in the local paper, consult its menu and find out from your penpal whether it would be a suitable place to take his family out for a meal. (CR I)

CR III and CR VII also show a concern with the issue of 'authenticity'.

Since, too, we had been anxious *dès le début* to select only those topic areas and those linguistic items which seemed relevant for children who might find themselves in France or Germany with a school party or parents, it seemed logical that our Speaking Test should only be concerned with situations which the children might encounter in such circumstances. (CR III)

The conventional kinds of cue adopted by many groups are role-play situations based on a cue-card in English (for example at the ticket office: ask if there is a train to Rouen; ask what time it leaves; buy a return ticket; and a number of questions in the foreign language on one or more specified topics: 'Tu as combien de frères ou de soeurs?' 'Tu fais quelles matières?'). Neither of these is new, both having been in existence in some public examinations for many years; they are well tried and they obviously achieve a degree of success when used at appropriate levels in the graded tests.

Serious doubts are expressed, however, about the authenticity of a situation in which the teacher pretends to be a greengrocer or (perhaps even less credibly) the pupil's friend. 'Can your teacher be your friend?' (CR I) – to which the apparent answer is 'no', with the result that, ideally, a test in which this pretence is made is not authentic and should be reconsidered. Given the rest of what is discussed in CR I, however, there is a strong possibility that, eventually, the answer could well be 'yes'. The solution to this problem adopted by some groups is to replace the teacher, in some cases, by another pupil, and also to make the language task itself more realistic by creating an information gap of the type mentioned in CR I above. There is enormous scope for development here, in terms of both testing and teaching resources and method. The fact remains, however, that a test will never be a 'real' situation, and that at some point the principle of simulation will have to be accepted: or so it seems at the moment.

Role-play cards present the additional problem of interpretation: if the instructions are in the foreign language, reading comprehension is being tested; if they are in English, as in most cases, the pupil has to transfer the instruction ('Pay the correct money') to the target language ('C'est combien? ... Voilà'). The higher the level of the test, the more difficult this skill becomes; attempts to overcome the problem have led some groups to try non-verbal stimuli, such as: pre-learnt instructions and simulation techniques, realia and visual cues, appreciably more 'global' assignments, and the 'information gap' mentioned above. All these have positive features, and deserve further development. Without being too pessimistic, however, it is worth bearing in mind the cautionary observations from Oxfordshire, one of the most experienced of the groups:

We have tried various formats, including pictures, diagrams, identity cards etc. but have often found that the more we tried to simplify administration, the more complex the test seemed to become to teacher as well as pupil. (CR VIII)

These observations constitute another timely warning that the perfect oral test may not be just round the corner.

Two final, disparate questions need to be asked about the use of non-verbal cues in the speaking test: first, how universally comprehensible are such cues in comparison with written text? Second, how beneficial will the backwash effect be on teaching styles? The answers may appear obvious, but we have little information available to prove them; one commissioned report suggests a number of ways in which teaching can reflect non-verbal testing forms, by using visuals in successive stages of: identification, reaction, sifting, completion and production of language (CR VI).

Transparency of task. CR IV uses the term 'transparency of task' to describe what is also considered as a leakage of information. The more global a task, the more suitable it is for leaking, with all the benefits of familiarity and practice this brings.

Such a procedure has several benefits. Firstly, student anxiety is reduced, the candidates have no fear of being given an assignment for which they are ill-prepared. Secondly, pupils will usually go home and 'rehearse' the tasks. This means that they will use their own time for the learning of materials already presented in class-time. If learning is the aim of teaching then this practice is beneficial. Thirdly, the interview can now be shortened. (CR IV)

The backwash effect is felt not only in language terms; the openness of the atmosphere created by this transparency contrasts favourably with the secrecy which still surrounds some of the examination boards. It is also liable to create a major area of conflict with the boards.

The problem of scoring. The assessing of pupil response in the oral test is probably the biggest single issue facing the graded test movement, given the high degree of subjectivity attached to it. An apparent break-through has been made, with the adoption of the concepts 'communicative competence/performance' and 'criterion-referencing'. In view of the short-lived nature of most previous breakthroughs in language teaching and learning, however, it is as well that thought is going into accommodating these ideas into teaching and testing practice. Andrew Harrison's report and the commissioned reports provide a good deal of food for thought. Instead of going over familiar arguments here, it is better to refer to the former for a discussion of criterion-referencing (Harrison, 1982, pp. 28–30). This is not the place to carry on the discussion – in the end the important point may not be whether oral/aural tests *are* completely criterion-referenced, but how the concept has been used to help them evolve. It has certainly contributed towards putting the act of communica-tion in a place of prime importance. Did it or did it not take place? Was the message (in the case of speaking tests) received and understood by the tester? The relevance of this criterion to the adoption and development of a series of language tasks is crucial, hence its oft-quoted importance to the graded tests. Already the tasks which pupils are asked to perform are clearly seen as real and as attainable, and pupils are correspondingly motivated.

But the idea of criterion-referencing itself does not solve the problem of what is acceptable. What are the criteria by which any utterance can be said to have achieved communication? Many of the reports mention this problem, with reference to attitude to error, level of performance, teacher experience, teacher flexibility and the standards of a 'sympathetic foreigner'. The definition of parameters along which language (whether it be short phrases or global utterances) can be assessed, the sub-sequent grading of these parameters, and their relative importance (accent, intonation, accuracy, fluency) are issues which need to be addressed, and to which the commissioned reports can make an important contribution. It may well be that the 'flash of lightning' with which communicative competence came on the scene has slightly blinded us to the fact that it is a subtle phenomenon, which needs to be handled carefully, and whose dimensions are many. Research may suggest that intuitive assessment by experienced testers of oral competence is as effective as analytical assessment,* but we still need to know on what that intuition is based. The question of scoring is also discussed in Chapter V.

One final comment on criterion-referencing: its yes/no approach is stunningly simple, but in order to convey the complex achievements of an individual, something much more subtle is required. This may be either a large block of information (such as a profile showing relative performance on a number of skills, achievements or attitudes), or a mere numerical assessment of achievements (a total percentage). The yes/no concept is binary, like the operations of a computer; but this simplicity should not be assumed to apply to the input (test forms), the processing (assessing) or the output (performance description) any more than it applies to the complex data which a computer is capable of handling.

Internal and external assessment. If tested as a discrete skill, listening is generally considered to be objective enough to be tested internally (by the teacher), with little or no outside supervision or moderation. In the case of speaking, however, or speaking and listening together, assessment is a more delicate matter, requiring a degree of objective and external involvement. As the oral tests will always be conducted by the teacher, or by a sympathetic outsider (i.e. not an 'external examiner'), this objectivity will be provided at the post-test level of moderation, when recordings of at least some tests will be made available. Similarly, a degree of confidentiality on precise test content will be necessary in order to ensure objectivity and fairness. In the case of continuous assessment, some groups, notably Lothian's Graded Levels of Achievement in Foreign Language Learning (GLAFLL), distinguish between a series of intermediate tests for which the school is entirely responsible (content, type, timing and assessing) and a smaller number of tests set externally and moderated. The latter tests are seen as summative, and are aimed at testing not the 'bits and pieces' of language – phrases, structures, functions – but overall global performance at communicating in a language in order to accomplish certain tasks not directly related to the syllabus. This approach has the advantage of retaining complete teacher control and flexibility over day-to-day progress and monitoring, whilst ensuring objectively that overall communicative aims are being met. It may also mean a proliferation of tests and checks.

---

* J. C. Francis, 'The reliability of two methods of marking oral tests in modern language examinations', *British Journal of Language Teaching*, vol. 19, no. 1, spring 1981; A. P. Dyson, *Oral Examining in French*, Modern Language Association, 1972.

Implications of growth

All the requirements mentioned so far in this chapter make plain the extent of physical and mental activity which have gone into the oral/aural tests, particularly the oral. The progress shown over the past few years is as impressive as the areas still to be covered are daunting.

The devising of tests such as these [multiple-skill tests of communicative ability] which go far beyond what foreign language teachers have attempted to date, is a daunting and ambitious task. (C R I)

Such development has brought the inevitable growing pains and areas of stress.

The stretching of resources. The success in developing realistic forms of oral/aural tests should not mask the great strain it has placed on personnel and resources. Further refinement and growth are inevitable, and this will increase that strain. It would be counter-productive to assume a limitless capacity of staff and finance, and unwise not to concentrate on 'software' (test content and procedures) and 'hardware' (the organization of working parties and local groups) which would use available capacity most efficiently.

The public examination boards. The fundamental differences between the norm-referenced, finely graded public examinations and the (would-be) criterion-referenced graded tests has been spelled out by Andrew Harrison (1982, pp. 30–32). The gap is perhaps likely to be bridged by the emergence of criteria to be applied nationally at 16 +, but the present state of affairs is exemplified in one of the commissioned reports:

[One problem is] the need to reconcile this style of testing with the generally accepted 'norm'. In a letter from the local CSE board this clash of examination personality is expressed thus: 'Panel members appreciated the thinking behind graded objectives in modern languages and that many candidates would score high marks in the examination. Two major problems were identified initially, one the difficulty of reconciling the graded test idea of achievement of a certain level of competence with that of the six categories or grades in the CSE, the other the relative demands of the proposed examination and their Mode I equivalents.' Despite fifty or more working groups currently active in the UK, ... the general level of acceptability remains comparatively low. (C R VII)

The question of whether the graded test movement should integrate with the public examination system, or go it alone, is well outside our brief. What has become apparent, however, is that the knowledge gained and improvements made in the areas of oral and aural examining form a formidable bank of expertise. This is already being fed into the system via the different graded test/examination board schemes; yet, in view of the present undecided nature of the proposed single-system 16+ examination, it seems that a far greater input could be made (in the areas, for example, of authenticity of listening texts, the variety of speaking situations and realistic and accurate assessment criteria).

The baby and the bathwater. Seen from the outside, many features of the graded tests – and particularly the commitment to exhaustive oral testing – may appear iconoclastic. Yet most of them have clear antecedents in previous and current teaching practice: the use of realia, topic and situation work, simulation, pair and group work, authentic texts, for example. Set against this background, such comparative newcomers as continuous assessment, unit credits, or even regular individual oral tests, seem less daunting. The information gathered for this report shows a vastly eclectic approach, adopting and adapting all that is best in past and present good practice. Not even the grammar baby (grammar, that is, used as an appropriate resource) has gone down the plughole with the bathwater.

The collaborative classroom. Now that 'the communicative classroom' is moving firmly into the list of conference topics, some of the implications of having communication as a main aim in language teaching need to be spelled out. Communication means learners (not just the teacher) speaking; and it means purposeful listening. Authentic communication means relating what is said and heard to the needs of learners, and this in turn means establishing those needs with the help of learners. As a result, not only will the classroom probably be a noisier place, but learners will be more involved in establishing, along with the teacher, what is to be studied. They will be partly responsible, through group work and self-access materials, for their own language development. The whole idea of learner-centred education implies that pupils will be more independent and cooperative, and that the classroom will be a more 'democratic' place.

Spreading the message. One of the reasons for the popularity of the graded tests – certainly amongst advisers and teacher-trainers – is the way in which they bring about in-service training. The awareness shown by teachers in the commissioned reports, of the complexities of oral/aural testing and communicative theory, is impressive and must be attributed to some extent to the intensity of discussion and development at group meetings. Given the contribution made by graded tests to INSET, it might be reasonable to expect that in-service resources could be made more available to groups, not to proselytize but to develop techniques which will be of use to all teachers.

IV. Analysis of selected tests

In addition to the collection of data via the questionnaire, commissioned reports and interviews, it was felt desirable to make at least a small-scale direct study of the test materials being produced for use in GOML schemes. This would enrich our description of the kind of testing currently taking place under the GOML banner. The main considerations of the study were:

How does the relationship between syllabus and assessment work out in practice in the oral/aural tests?

What weighting is given to listening (L) and speaking (S)?

Are the skills being assessed separately (in a discrete mode) or together (in an integrative mode)?

Do the tests sample pupil mastery of some defined syllabus (however defined) and/or assess pupils' global communicative proficiency in the foreign language?

How far have concepts of 'criterion referencing' penetrated into the scoring systems of the tests?

How much weight is being given to continuous assessment, in comparison with summative assessment?

Collecting the tests

We did not have the resources to make anything like a complete study of all current GOML scheme tests. We therefore decided to study a limited number of tests, selecting the projects to be included in an attempt to maximize the variety of test types looked at. In April 1982 the following groups kindly agreed to send us copies of their French tests at Level 1. It is on these that the analysis is based.*

*The tests looked at have been produced at varying times between 1977 and 1982, and some of them are currently under revision. However our aim was to study tests *actually in use* in 1982, and we understand this was the case for this group of tests.

Belfast Graded Tests in French (Level 1)
City of Birmingham Graded Examinations in French (Level 1)
Cumbria/Lancashire Graded Proficiency Tests in Modern Languages (Level 1, French)
East Midlands Graded Assessment Syllabus (Level 1, French)
Eclair Graded Tests (Level 1)*
Lothian Region Graded Levels of Achievement in Foreign Language Learning (GLAFLL) (Stage 1)
Oxfordshire Modern Language Achievement Certificate (OMLAC) (Level 1, French)
South West Region French Credit 3 (first edition)
Scottish Central Committee for Modern Languages (SCCML) Tour de France Project (Stage 1)
York Area French Proficiency Test (Level 1).

Analysing the tests

A checklist of points to look for was established, as a guide to the examination of each set of oral/aural test materials. Where mixed-skill tests occurred in which listening and/or speaking were combined with reading and/or writing, all test items involving oral/aural skills were examined.

Using the checklist as a guide, a detailed, standardized description was written about each set of test materials. These descriptions, which total thirty-three pages, form the basis of the following discussion. Obviously, the ten test batteries, selected on a non-random basis, do not form a 'representative' sample of all GOML Level 1 tests. In the following discussion therefore, the aim is to illustrate the *variety* of approaches being adopted on such questions as skill definition and syllabus design, choice of item types and scoring systems, within the GOML movement, rather than to seek any sort of common denominator.

Syllabus

All the assessment schemes looked at were associated with some form of defined syllabus, except one (the York scheme). These varied in length from the 78-page GLAFLL syllabus (admittedly covering Stages 1–3) to the five-page Birmingham syllabus. The two assessment schemes associated with actual courses (Eclair and Tour de France) took the

* The *Eclair* series, by the Inner London Education Authority, is published by Mary Glasgow Publications, 1980.

coursebook syllabus as the assessment syllabus. The associated syllabuses were defined in a wide variety of terms. Most specified 'topic areas' in some form (e.g. 'personal information', 'shopping', 'at the café'), and most had shorter or longer lexical and structural lists of actual foreign-language (FL) items. But for some groups these lists *were* the syllabus (e.g. Belfast and Birmingham); for others they were merely exponents (optional or compulsory) of functional/notional lists, which appeared to constitute the core of the syllabus (South West, GLAFLL). There were also cases where chunks of structure had been given functional labels (e.g. East Midlands, and parts of Tour de France syllabus); in these cases it seemed that structure remained the primary basis.

In most syllabuses an attempt was made to distinguish items specified for productive and for receptive competence (see p. 59), though this principle was not always consistently carried through in the syllabus (and sometimes ignored in associated tests). Most seemed intended for about a year's schoolwork (GLAFLL being an exception); there was striking variation in the absolute amount of language material included. For example, the Tour de France, East Midlands and South West syllabuses seriously get to grips with the verb system, while Eclair and Oxfordshire do not. Target populations do vary, but some of the lighter syllabuses are intended for all abilities, some of the heavier for the 'less able'.

General rationale for assessment schemes

The rationale for a scheme will generally be expressed in its specified aims or objectives. Some projects provide no explicit rationale, at least not within the actual test materials. Of those that do, most express it in more or less behavioural terms, for example:

The stage tests are ... a kind of 'dipstick' reading of a pupil's potential to *cope with authentic, communicative situations* in the foreign language. (GLAFLL)

At Level 1 ... candidates must *demonstrate an ability to deal successfully in French* with the listening, reading and speaking required to: ask the way and understand directions; shop for food ... (York Level 1)

Others provide a rationale concerned with motivation, e.g.:

To give both teachers and pupils *a useful, enjoyable programme* of work in the early stages of learning French. (Belfast)

To *promote confidence* in the use of French for the purposes of communication in specified topic areas. (East Midlands)*

* In all these cases, the emphases have been added subsequently by us.

Links between syllabuses and assessment schemes

In some schemes it is made clear that the intention has been to develop *achievement* tests, to evaluate pupils' mastery of the elements of the defined language syllabus. Belfast and Eclair both state explicitly that 'only items from the syllabus' will be tested; in the Birmingham and South West test batteries, study of the tests makes it clear that virtually all test items are sampling the syllabus lists.

In other schemes, however, one or more tests in the total test battery get away from syllabus-sampling, and include 'integrative' tasks for which mastery of the defined syllabus is helpful but not essential. GLAFLL, Tour de France and OMLAC contain examples of this type of test (see below for more detailed descriptions).

Generally, those schemes with a 'continuous assessment' element in the total assessment pattern seem to sample the defined syllabus most fully. East Midlands and Birmingham have organized their syllabus into topics which are also intended to form the basis of actual teaching units, and each of these units has its own achievement test sampling the relevant syllabus section. The OMLAC scheme also includes a 'Progress Card' for continuous assessment of topic mastery, with groups of test items for each syllabus topic. Schools in the GLAFLL scheme are expected to develop their own syllabus-sampling achievement tests for purposes of continuous assessment (and marks from these go towards the final assessment total); and Tour de France also has tests systematically sampling the syllabus for each unit of work, though in this case such tests are purely diagnostic. Thus, even the schemes whose tests include integrative tasks as opposed to syllabus-sampling items have not on this account abandoned syllabus definition, or the attempt to get pupils to master a defined syllabus.

Oral/aural test types

All the Level 1 schemes under consideration place great importance on the assessment of oral/aural ability. Each test battery includes at least two sections assessing some aspect of oral/aural competence. The following summary list shows which schemes have discrete-skill listening (L) tests, discrete-skill speaking (S) tests, interactive (L/S) tests, and tests involving L and/or S with another skill (such as reading, R):

Belfast	L test, L/S test
Birmingham	L items, S items, L/S items (all scattered through 5 mixed-skill 'topic' tests)
Cumbria/Lancashire	L test, S test
East Midlands	L/S tests ('topic' tests), L/R test
Eclair	L test, S test
GLAFLL	L test, L/S test, L/R test
OMLAC	L/R test, S test (Progress Card), L/S test
South West	L test, S test
Tour de France	L test, L/S test
York	L test, L/S test.

Thus the balance between discrete and mixed skills is fairly even. Eight schemes include some kind of discrete-skill listening test, while seven test speaking at least partly in conjunction with listening, and five test speaking as a discrete skill. The L/R label shown for three schemes above actually covers two very different test types. GLAFLL and OMLAC include one or two 'narrative sequences' in their test batteries, with foreign language listening *or* reading items embedded at intervals in a story line expressed in English. East Midlands on the other hand sets a test in which pupils hear an FL narrative, and must match sections of the narrative with printed FL sentences summarizing the information. This is the only instance in any of these schemes of a mixed-skill task involving reading (apart from FL cues on role-play cards in some L/S tests).

Listening tests

The types of listening test found in the various schemes may be placed on a scale relative to the complexity of the comprehension skills demanded. The scale is as follows:

1 Recognition of isolated discrete language items (words or phrases) drawn from the defined syllabus.

2 Recognition of similar syllabus items, contained in longer passages composed of other material drawn from the syllabus.

3 Recognition of syllabus items contained in foreign-language material *not* drawn from the syllabus.

4 'Integrative' comprehension skills: gist extraction, inference, collation of redundant information, discriminating among 'false clues' in a longer passage, including non-syllabus material.

Listening tests (or test items) falling on all points of this scale are to be found among the schemes under discussion. The Belfast, Birmingham and Cumbria/Lancashire listening tests are all or mainly of the first type, Tour de France and OMLAC (listening items in L/R test) preponderantly of the second type. The Belfast scheme expressed an intention of constructing tests of the third type, but do not do so in the battery provided at Level 1; most items in the Eclair listening test are of this third type.

The GLAFLL listening test, and part of the South West test, are the only substantial examples in the schemes being looked at here of assessment of comprehension at point 4 on the scale of complexity. The South West listening test includes five items involving gist extraction from texts (on audiotape) containing part specified, part non-specified material. (This test also includes five items testing the ability to match particular phrases with the general notions of which they are exponents.) The GLAFLL test also involves gist extraction from 'enriched' recorded dialogues, in which two speakers debate/negotiate/comment on the information the pupil is required to identify.

Thus at Level 1, most schemes appear to interpret 'listening comprehension' in terms of the recognition of specified syllabus items, in contexts of varying complexity. In most listening tests, some form of contextualization for the discrete foreign-language stimuli is provided (normally in English). The commonest types of pupil response are English multiple choice (Eclair), multiple choice in the foreign language (East Midlands), copying names from a map (Belfast), physical response (e.g. to 'Lève-toi!' Birmingham), 'forced choice' matching of utterances with printed English sentences (South West).

Listening tests seem to be universally administered on a whole-class basis. Those with more elaborate stimuli have a taped presentation, others require the teacher to read stimulus material. Scoring is normally 'objective', with 'model answers' in English occasionally provided for written responses. Items are scored individually, and marks are summed to give an aggregate score.

Speaking tests

The distinction is again found between discrete and mixed-skill testing in the speaking tests. Five of the test schemes include tests or items assessing speaking as an isolated skill. In some of these, pupils must produce discrete syllabus items in response to a non-contextualized English stimulus (some Birmingham items, all items in the Cumbria/Lancashire speaking test). In the remainder, pupils must produce utterances from the defined syllabus, in contextualized question/answer exchanges or role-play dialogues. In the Birmingham items, and some Eclair items, a specified structural item must be produced. In the other tests a choice of exponents is allowed, for specified functions/notions. Contextualization and stimuli are again in English; while the teacher is usually required to play the other role in such test items, the English scripting of the required pupil utterances means that the pupil can complete the task successfully without taking any account of what the teacher says. Such tasks are *pseudo-*interactive; it is not always clear that the test-writers appreciate that only the speaking skill is being tested in such items. Some Birmingham items, the Eclair test, the O M L A C continuous assessment scheme, and the South West test are of this type. All have some form of 'cue card' for the pupil, with English stimuli (Eclair also has pictures).

On the question of prompting (see pp. 32–4 and 63–6), only two of the schemes possessing speaking tests give advice to the class teacher (who is always envisaged as administering the tests, on an individual basis). Eclair provides a choice of scripted prompts in the foreign language, South West suggests 'one rephrasing' of the teacher's foreign-language question which accompanies the cue card prompt in English.

The scoring of tests is another important issue covered elsewhere. Pupil utterances in all single-skill tests reviewed here are assessed individually. Four out of the five tests rate individual utterances on a 2- or 3-point scale; brief scale-point descriptions are provided, which take account of such features as intelligibility and accuracy. The Birmingham system awards one or two marks per utterance, depending on the complexity of the structure required. The Eclair system, in addition to rating individual utterances, requires retrospective global rating of pupil performance on a 10-point scale. Five bands on this scale are described taking account of such features as fluency, readiness to initiate, pronunciation, and 'communicative skill'. It seems relevant to ask whether pupil performance on only fifteen items eliciting individual specified language functions can provide substantive evidence on some of these dimensions.

'Integrative' listening/speaking tests

As has been seen, seven of the schemes under consideration had some form of assessment for interactive oral/aural skills. These most often took the form of an individual oral interview with the class teacher. In O M L A C, and in the East Midlands continuous assessment subtests ('assessment blocks'), pairs of pupils interact with each other, and the teacher observes/evaluates. In GLAFLL, a teacher–pupil and a pupil–pupil task is required of each pupil. (GLAFLL also proposes using the foreign language assistant as interlocutor in the teacher–pupil tasks.)

Two item types dominate these integrative tests. One is the individual question/answer exchange, which may be contextualized (as in East Midlands 'assessment blocks') or not. In the Belfast, Birmingham and York schemes, such exchanges are the only integrative element in the test battery. (Belfast and York also have role-play tasks, but these are scripted in such a way as to test speaking only, like those discussed in the previous section.) In all three cases the teacher initiates all such exchanges, and the pupil responds. In the East Midlands scheme such exchanges are also the only integrative element in the continuous assessment tests, but in this case the exchanges take place between pairs of pupils. Pupils exchange the initiating role between test tasks (which consist of five exchanges), but not within them. The Tour de France scheme also includes such exchanges as one element in its listening/speaking test.

The other mixed-skill item type is to be found in the two Scottish schemes (GLAFLL and Tour de France) and in OMLAC. This is the *unscripted* role-play or 'simulated negotiation' task. In GLAFLL and Tour de France, the teacher interacts with the candidate in such tasks; in GLAFLL also, and in OMLAC, pairs of pupils perform them together.

The interesting point about these tasks is that they are the nearest approach in the Level 1 test batteries to the elicitation of *communicative* performance from pupils. They are like the scripted role-plays previously discussed, in having a (simulated) context and stated purpose (if only of the 'buy an ice cream', 'make a date' type); they differ from them in also containing an element of unpredictability, and in the necessity to take account of what the other person says, in devising one's next utterance. This point is taken up again on pp. 64–5.

The tasks proposed in these tests (OMLAC, GLAFLL, Tour de France) relate in all cases to a specified topic area of the syllabus. Knowing the defined language syllabus is therefore likely to help pupil performance, but only in the GLAFLL teacher–pupil task is there any requirement that the pupil realize any specific syllabus element (some functions are listed in this case, as necessary components of the pupil's contribution to the conversation). As the Tour de France Teacher's Notes put it, pupils are expected to 'draw on anything they can think of to solve the (communication) problem' in performing these tasks. The tasks involve such things as finding out personal information, engaging in instrumental negotiation (offering, ordering), and/or phatic interaction. In some tasks pupils are supplied with information not known to their partners (e.g. in the OMLAC tasks, where pupils are issued with cue cards having different information as the basis for a paired conversation).

Where the teacher is involved in these role-play tasks (in Tour de France and in GLAFLL), s/he is given limited guidance on his/her own behaviour: in both cases the suggestion is for teachers 'to see themselves as intelligent native speakers, aware that they are conversing with .... foreigners' (GLAFLL). Teacher-style prompting is thus implicitly ruled out.

Where the teacher is not involved directly, but has a monitoring/ evaluating role (OMLAC and GLAFLL), no guidance on prompting is given. However, the GLAFLL notes suggest that where a pupil–pupil conversation breaks down, the teacher can step in and ask additional questions of individuals; this obviously changes the nature of the task. Surprisingly, in view of the evident possibility of doubt about the effect of one learner's performance on another, neither scheme has much to say about how to react to it (though OMLAC reminds teachers this is only an experimental element in the test battery, and permits it to count for very little in the overall mark scheme).

Pupil global performance on these tasks is in all three cases rated on a scale (four points in OMLAC, three in the other two schemes). In Tour de France, performance on each of three tasks is rated separately; in OMLAC and GLAFLL, performance on each of two tasks is rated together. Scale-point descriptions are provided in each case, taking account of a variety of dimensions of performance, with an emphasis on communicative effectiveness.

The Tour de France listening and speaking test rates pupil performance on the four question/answer exchanges in the same way as on the global tasks. The other tests of this type score or rate pupil utterances individually: York rates them on a four-point scale, taking account of a number of performance dimensions (of the types mentioned in Chapter V, pp. 68–9), while the rest score them on a yes/no basis. For East Midlands, the essential criterion is intelligibility; for Belfast and Birmingham, it appears to be structural accuracy. Utterances containing errors can gain maximum scores in both the York and East Midlands schemes.

The rating of integrative performances on listening and speaking tests is well recognized as presenting problems of reliability. There is only slight evidence in the actual test materials made available of efforts to improve reliability through moderation and tester training. Some schemes recommend recording at least a sample of tests, for purposes of moderation, but if tester training is taking place on a wide scale, it is going unrecognized in test notes and instructions. In fact, we have other evidence to suggest that some projects do devote considerable efforts to this; GLAFLL, for example, makes a training package available to school departments which includes specimen test performances at different levels. Only the York scheme recommends recording of all tests routinely, for retrospective scoring; the rest assume scoring simultaneous with test administration. The York procedure would seem to offer possibilities for cooperative scoring by groups of teachers, and within-school moderation, as well as providing data for across-school comparisons. The question of moderating is further discussed in Chapter V, p. 69.

Standards, pass marks and criterion referencing

Two of the schemes reviewed here provided no information on their procedures for determining 'pass' levels (Belfast and Cumbria/Lancashire). Among those providing such information, only the Tour de France and Eclair schemes make any explicit claim in their test materials that their scoring procedures are criterion-referenced. Informally, other project leaders have argued that this is the case for their tests, but even for these two schemes, it may be asked what basis there is for their explicit claim. Criterion referencing implies acceptance of two basic principles: first, that the pass level, or criterion to be met, be described explicitly, in behavioural terms. To say the criterion is '50 per cent on our speaking test', does not meet this condition, though to say '90 per cent on our speaking test' may do so, if the test itself has a clearly defined behavioural specification, which then effectively serves as the criterion. Second, pupil performance on the test must be assessed in relation to the knowledge and skills detailed in the criterion performance description, and not in relation to the performance of other pupils.

The Eclair scoring system in fact runs counter to both of these principles. While the listening and speaking tests are accompanied by a fairly explicit description of target competence, the actual pass levels are set so low (below 50 per cent for both tests) that a 'pass' cannot be assumed to mean a fully adequate performance in terms of the description. The reasons for this low 'pass' level turns out to be the wish that over 90 per cent of all Inner London Education Authority (ILEA) pupils should experience success at Level 1. This concern for motivation through success is praiseworthy, but it seems to have led here to the clear reintroduction of norm-referencing principles. Here as elsewhere (see Chapter V, 'Setting the level') the two apparent extremes of norm referencing and criterion referencing are seen to overlay and interact to a degree which in theory seems unlikely.

Grading (further discussed in Chapter V) again shows a variety of approaches by the groups. Tour de France, like Eclair, reports separately on pupil performance on its various tests, and does not produce any aggregate single score. For the listening test, a 'pass' level of 70 per cent is set. For the integrative test, consisting of four interview tasks, pupils must achieve an 'effective' grade on at least three tasks in order to be graded 'effective' overall. The 70 per cent pass level brings the necessary pupil competence considerably nearer to the overall target competences described for the listening test. Additionally, as we have seen, the 'grade' levels used in scoring listening and speaking test tasks themselves have explicit behavioural descriptions, so that a check backwards should tell us what the Stage 1 'pass' pupil knows/can do in relation to identifiable tasks. The basic Tour de France scheme thus seems closer to a true criterion-referenced system, though the listening test pass level might still seem a bit on the low side. The attempt to differentiate at the top end of performance and establish a 'credit' level has a shakier basis, however, at least as far as listening is concerned; all that distinguishes 'effective' and 'highly effective' listening is 15 percentage points. The 'highly effective' award works better in the listening and speaking tests, where the credit is won by reaching the highest grade level on all four tasks.

The GLAFLL scheme is the only other one among those reviewed here (apart possibly from East Midlands, who provided little information on this issue) which does not aggregate scores from the various tests into one grand total score. To get a GLAFLL Level 1 award, pupils must achieve the most basic specified 'Level of Performance' (LOP) 1 on the integrative listening and speaking test. They must also achieve a score of 70 per cent on the internal school Waystage tests (not reviewed here, but intended to sample the language syllabus) and listening and reading stage tests. The GLAFLL scheme thus is not dissimilar from the Tour de France scheme on this issue. It also awards Stage 1 with 'credit', for which LOP 2 plus a higher percentage performance on the other tests are necessary.

The East Midlands scheme intends to award Level 1 passes either in 'talking' (i.e. oral/aural proficiency) alone, or in talking/reading/writing. The remaining schemes produce a single aggregate score, by summing pupil scores on their various continuous assessment schemes and/or summative tests, sometimes altering the weighting of different test performances in the final total. (South West multiplies speaking scores by 2, to bring speaking *up* to a one-third weighting in the aggregate score; OMLAC divides Progress Card speaking scores by 2, to bring speaking *down* to a one-third weighting.) OMLAC uses its Progress Card scores twice, once as an entry qualification for the summative tests (a 67 per cent pass level is necessary for this), and once as an element in the final score for award of a certificate. This weighting process sometimes has bizarre results, as in the OMLAC scheme, where the elaborate integrative test with its paired speaking tasks ends up contributing a possible *two marks* to the total aggregate score of 60 marks.

The Birmingham, South West and York schemes all have a predetermined pass level stated as a percentage of their total aggregate scores (67, 57 and 70 per cent respectively). OMLAC and East Midlands both determine the pass score retrospectively, in the light of pupil performance on the tests; in OMLAC it apparently varies annually, depending on the ability levels, as perceived by teachers, of the pupil population taking the tests that year. OMLAC thus represents the most thorough application of norm-referencing principles of all the schemes reviewed here.

Certification

Too few actual certificates were sent to us to allow for any extended comment on this subject, also referred to in Chapter V. Most schemes obviously have them, and value them greatly as important motivational elements in the scheme. Those we did see (GLAFLL Record of Achievement, York Certificate, Tour de France Report Card) include praiseworthy attempts to communicate, briefly and in non-technical terms, the nature of the pupil competence being recognized through the award. Informal evidence from the Scottish projects at least suggests that parents and pupils value such descriptions greatly, and find them meaningful. An obvious possible pitfall, from which the certificates seen are not completely free, is to describe the meaning of Level 1 success in somewhat inflated terms. But how to combine modesty with economy and maximum information is a difficult problem.

Some conclusions

All the Level 1 schemes reviewed here are making serious attempts to assess and report on pupils' oral/aural ability at an early stage. Radically different understanding of what is possible in the early days of foreign language learning clearly underlies the range of schemes. Some limit their efforts, through their syllabus and test schemes, to trying to ensure pupil mastery of a limited set of discrete language items. Others are aiming, even for Level 1, at the development of a more open-ended communicative proficiency, for which defined syllabus lists are only an interim support. Paradoxically these more ambitious projects also tend to have more extensively defined syllabuses than the first group. The tests reviewed here thus have different general goals; it is sensible only to enquire whether they actually match their respective goals (i.e. actually test the kind of pupil competence they claim to be interested in), not to argue that all schemes should have the same goals.

Nonetheless many of the schemes would appear to have similar problems, and a number of areas can be identified where research and development work on assessment procedures could be of general benefit. These complement, and at times overlap, the areas picked out in Chapter VII.

The first general issue concerns the relationship of the syllabus with the various discrete-point tests, whether of listening or of speaking. Almost all such tests attempt to sample some defined syllabus; how to do this systematically is clearly an outstanding problem. In many of the tests studied here, the syllabus had been sampled somewhat haphazardly, with over-representation of some syllabus areas at the expense of others. Number, time and price systems often appeared over-represented, for example. The provision of multiple versions of some tests, with different versions providing a different sampling of the same syllabus, improves the picture obtained of overall performance of groups of pupils, but does not increase confidence in the sampling of any one individual's mastery of the target syllabus. One way of improving sampling is of course to increase the length of tests taken by each individual; but practical constraints intervene, presumably accounting for the extreme brevity of most syllabus-sampling speaking tests (see Chapter II, question 13.5). The projects which include systematic continuous assessment in their schemes seem to have found one of the better solutions to this problem. Their 'coverage' of the language syllabus as far as speaking is concerned was generally better than that of those who left all oral assessment until the summative stage.

The administration and scoring of open-ended, integrative test tasks, which appear essential in order to assess communicative proficiency even at Level 1, is another major area where additional developmental work, and additional resource support for teachers administering the tests, seem necessary. None of the schemes currently using such tasks has had the resources to conduct a major systematic evaluation of their reliability and validity. The various rating systems proposed for scoring pupil performance seem in particular need of such investigation. These issues are much discussed, but must remain in doubt until a lot more work has been done. We can dodge this problem at Level 1, perhaps, by excluding such tests from our test batteries. But the issue will still face us at higher levels.

The issue of criterion referencing and its applicability in schemes for the assessment of elementary foreign language competence is another major 'problem' issue. It would appear that many GOML schemes have not yet come to grips with the issue, and some still seem unaware of the norm-referencing/criterion-referencing debate. Again many theoretical and practical questions in this area are unanswered. Yet the arguments for a move in this direction remain compelling, particularly in view of the clear commitment of the projects reviewed here to redefining the general objectives of modern languages teaching in communicative terms.

V. Oral/aural tests in action: a step-by-step guide

It is apparent that the setting of suitable oral and aural tests is a daunting task. On the one hand, the number of possible tests available, and the complexity of some of the theoretical and practical issues to be taken into account, are initially overwhelming. On the other, the dynamism with which testing theory is developing (after what must, in the context of other subject areas, be a relatively slow start) can create a sense of vertigo in all but the most committed professionals. This chapter represents an attempt to distil the experience of established GOML groups. It draws in particular on a series of interviews conducted during the summer of 1982. The technique of gathering information verbally was considered very appropriate for a report on oral/aural skills. It also proved most effective.*

This chapter aims to trace in roughly chronological progression those decisions which groups may or should face in devising a suitable strategy towards oral and aural work. Local conditions will, as always, be decisive for the final outcome, so possible solutions offered here are suggestive rather than prescriptive. The main questions are those concerned with test type and content; administrative requirements are only discussed when they are directly related to the former.

Agreeing motives

In addition to the general dissatisfaction felt within the graded objectives movement at the idea of the 'grand-slam' examination at 16+, with all its negative effects on language teaching, there is a more specific objection

---

* The people interviewed were: David Bolton, Huntington School, York; Keith Gordon and Liz Roselman, Oxford Modern Language Achievement Certificate; David Peacock, Cumbria/Lancashire; Roy Dunning, School of Education, University of Leicester, East Midlands Graded Assessment Feasibility Study; John Clark, Graded Levels of Achievement in Foreign Language Learning (Lothian); Nicki Lees, East Midlands Graded Assessment Feasibility Study; Do Coyle, Bigwood School, Nottingham (East Midlands); and Tom Garside, Weald School, Billingshurst (West Sussex).

to the relatively low status traditionally afforded to the skills of listening and speaking – the two skills crucial for interaction in a foreign language. This lack of importance could be attributed to difficulty in designing reliable tests (particularly in the case of speaking) and no doubt accounts for the paltry nature of many listening tests and the flimsy description and execution of speaking tests.

Any reaction to this unsatisfactory state of affairs, and its stultifying effect on oral and aural work in the classroom, will require, therefore, a commitment to the importance of the spoken language in life, in the classroom and in testing schemes. Speaking and listening tests will have to receive suitably substantial weighting; tests will have to be devised of a reliability to match this weighting, and ways will have to be found to use spoken language increasingly, and for *real* purposes, in the classroom. This is no slight commitment, but without it, it would be prudent to do no more than simply to liven up one's present teaching techniques with as much 'son et lumière' as resources will permit.

Setting the level

The form and level of difficulty of the tests will depend on the learners for whom they are intended and the type of teaching they have received. In conventional examinations the idea of success has been discarded in favour of fine grading of performance (of failure, some would claim). And yet there is little point in teaching the conveying and understanding of spoken language for the purpose of getting a message across if tests are devised at a level such that a majority of the message is misunderstood or not conveyed. The next decision to take is therefore that in the oral and aural tests the majority of learners will achieve successful communication in the majority of cases. This must be a more useful educational tool than a mere rank order based on a wide spread of marks.

The exact definition of 'majority' when deciding the degree of success to be achieved in the tests reveals a considerable range of attitude within existing groups (Chapter IV), not so much in terms of percentage of successful candidates (generally around 90 per cent) as in overall score, which varies from 50 per cent, or slightly less, to 70 per cent or more.

When deciding the level of success to be expected, it should be borne in mind that criterion referencing requires that the level of *performance* required for a pass be established, and not the percentage of candidates. The two are obviously related, and the purists will certainly object to any use of norm referencing, but the most salutory effect of criterion referencing is that the need to set realistic standards, appropriate to the majority of the ability range, requires a very careful scrutiny of learner potential and of the level and content of any test. In other words, the setting of criteria must be based on wide experience of the norm.

Finding the right language

Once it has been decided that the spoken language used in the tests, and therefore in teaching, must be relevant and have a purpose, it is clear that structural grammar, however broken down, and however ingeniously exemplified, cannot form the sole or central basis of syllabus and course design. We have traditionally accepted the progression from definite article to imperfect subjunctive as the groundwork for our teaching but the field is now open for a whole new rationale. In order to establish that rationale, the most obvious course is to indulge in a comprehensive needs analysis. Not only do we have to consider *why* a language is being learnt, we have to establish precisely the physical situations, the people involved, the purpose, the mode and register, as well as the generally accepted structural and vocabulary content. Native wit and experience will play an encouragingly large part in this operation, which is bound to throw up some surprising results, so hidebound are some of our assumptions about language. Recent findings in the fields of psycholinguistics and sociolinguistics will also be useful. One extremely beneficial side-effect of needs analysis is that it can only properly be done in consultation with the customers: the pupils. There is evidence that such interaction between teacher and pupils in a collaborative venture has a highly motivating effect, both psychologically and in terms of validity of results. The learner's natural urge to communicate is thus harnessed, rather than shackled by prescriptive language drilling. There are two main likely outcomes to this step, which could be expressed in terms of themes and skills:

THEMES
It is likely to emerge that spoken language will be concerned with 'surviving' in a number of formal or semi-formal situations (way-finding, bank, restaurant, etc.), and/or with conversation with friends or family on a range of personal topics (family, school, leisure, work, etc.).

SKILLS
Purposeful listening will not have much to do with funny stories from books, meandering conversations or long monologues from literary

sources. It is more likely to consist of public announcements such as in airports, and railway stations, news items and responses to questions and requests of the type made in the 'survival situations' mentioned above. Speaking activities will consist of getting what you want (transactional language) in the survival situations, and of taking part in a personal conversation (social, informational and attitudinal language). This rudimentary analysis is open to refinement and to debate. It also ignores for the moment the question of whether the skills of listening and speaking are separable (to be dealt with under 'Discrete or mixed skills?'), and it fails to consider the relative importance of the different themes and skills at successive levels – a decision likely to be taken according to local experience and judgement, which in turn are importantly influenced by conditions and by personalities.

Describing your language

The proliferation of syllabuses currently available both within and outside the graded objectives movement, and the polemic which attaches to syllabus definition, throw into relief the relatively imperfect state of the art of describing what language is, and how it behaves. But now is the time to throw off the shackles of Latin grammar, and to try, however imperfectly, to put down what it is we are attempting to teach and test. Not only will this necessitate a clear thinking-out of objectives, but explicit syllabus definition will be increasingly necessary as the members of a GOML group increase, and as newcomers need a clear statement of those objectives which previously were no more than unstated common attitudes, evolved and elaborated by working together.

The metalanguage of communicative theory – better known as 'jargon', and increasingly used by the mentors of foreign language teachers – will have to be mastered by leaders of groups, at least, and preferably by all members. On the other hand, if real communication is to be achieved between teachers, it should be used sparingly. The brief glossary which forms Appendix B is a modest attempt to clarify some of the terms most commonly used and abused.

AIMS

An explicit statement of aims may refer to all or some of the wide range possible: the provision of an experience which is enjoyable, relevant or successful; the teaching of specified language skills (listening, speaking, reading, writing); the inculcation of attitudes of understanding, tolerance, sympathy or critical admiration towards the foreign language speakers and their culture; 'education for leisure'; an understanding and appreciation of the way in which language works; or simply a mastery of some of the skills of communication at an appropriate level (which could be spelled out in terms of many of the foregoing characteristics). The aims expressed will to some extent reflect emphasis placed on short-term goals such as rote-learning and long-term goals such as character development.

TYPES OF SYLLABUS

Three major types of syllabus have been found useful in existing schemes, the individual elements of which can be re-combined in a wide variety of ways. The three main types are based on:

Situations and topics. The 'survival situations', most of which denote a physical location (shops, post office, etc.), pre-determine the choice of a certain number of structures and vocabulary, whilst the conversational topics are used to select the framework and the lexical and grammatical basis for the language of face-to-face conversation with a foreign language speaker who is, or is about to be, a friend. The choice of language to be understood and manipulated within these limits is a matter for negotiation, and usually takes the form of structures, phrases and words most likely to be used. These may be listed simply under each topic, or also as a comprehensive vocabulary or grammatical structure list.

Functions and notions. Functions express the purpose for which language is used (agreeing, persuading, requesting); notions are the concepts (time, number, availability, cause and effect) which can be expressed by language. Much work has been done within the Council of Europe Modern Languages Project on defining the notions and functions most likely to be needed by learners of different European languages. But it must be admitted that our knowledge of exactly how they help the foreign language teacher is still restricted. Such a syllabus may offer a relatively accurate description of how language works, but as with other syllabuses, considerable effort is required to make it applicable to the teaching situation.

'Communicative areas'. This is an expression used by OMLAC to describe an approach common to other groups. The areas are:

1 Establishing and maintaining social contacts
2 Expressing opinions
3 Getting around
4 Arranging accommodation

5 Obtaining goods
6 Obtaining services
7 Talking about past events and experiences
8 Making plans

The range of activity covered by each area means that it can be more precisely defined at each level, with an increasing number of sub-divisions and exponents. More importantly, perhaps, the aim is also to show that physical location (as in a situation-based syllabus) is too rigid a way of describing language, the successful use of which requires a large degree of flexibility and transferability from one area to another.

A decision as to which, if any, of these three main types of description will be used as a basis will again depend on local experience and perceptions. The main aim should be to achieve, by any combination of elements, the most suitable (accurate) description of the language and of target levels of performance which the majority of members think will help them towards the style of teaching they have decided to adopt. It is worth remembering, however, that no description of a language will, alone, be adequate as a basis for the learning of it.

DEGREE OF DEFINITION

Defined syllabuses, like defined objectives, are generally accepted as being valuable and necessary. Until recently, the more precise a definition was, the more useful it was considered to be. There is a danger, however, that the writing-out in the syllabus of lists of phrases, structures and words, may lead to the teaching of these in their raw form, and their regurgitation in the oral examination. The successful 'parroting' of a number of set phrases in a limited number of defined situations may be seen as a satisfactory short-term aim, but by itself it cannot constitute communicative proficiency. The learner must also be equipped to cope in some way with unforeseen communicative needs, such as understanding the native speaker who hasn't read the defined syllabus, or getting the message across when a precise term is not known.

PROGRESSING THROUGH THE LEVELS

The increase in oral/aural skills to be mastered at each level can be expressed in terms of extra topics/situations, notions/functions or 'communicative areas'. At the same time, the effectiveness with which communication can be achieved within previous areas can be increased by adding to the number of exponents available for each one, or the number and complexity of tasks to be performed within each one.

All GOML groups assume that skills acquired at one level are automatically retained at the next. Some groups use as a basis for selection the kind of language needed to cope with increasingly complex situations, from day-trips to the foreign country, to a stay in a foreign family.

RECEPTIVE AND PRODUCTIVE SPEECH

In the detailed listing of language to be used, it will be important to distinguish between the language it is considered the pupil will be expected to say (productive) and that which s/he will be expected to understand (receptive). The two groups will often present very different characteristics (for example: in a railway station, asking for and understanding departure times and listening to announcements), and receptive language will be more extensive than productive. Allowance for the 'gist' understanding of words and phrases not specifically set out in the syllabus should also be considered – although the extent to which coping strategies of this kind are currently practised and tested is uneven.

BALANCE OF SKILLS

It is generally considered that understanding speech is easier than speaking. If this is agreed, then there is a case for increasing the weighting of listening in earlier levels, and of adding to the amount of speaking to be done at later levels. If speaking tasks are then set so that they also test listening ability, this will mean no effective decrease in the importance of listening.

Discrete or mixed skills?

This question, which inevitably occurs in many parts of this book, must be tackled directly. Needs analysis will probably have shown that certain types of listening (notably listening to announcements and to the media) can be quite separate from speaking, but that speaking rarely occurs without the need to understand at least something of what is replied. Ideally, then, speaking tests should entail the need to show that the reponse to the learner's own speech has been understood. Thus account will be taken of what is replied in any of a number of ways, by noting down facts learnt, by responding either physically, or by adjusting a course of action (e.g. buying pears if apples aren't available). The decision to be made is whether, at any of the levels, the complications caused by this interaction for tester and tested are justified by the need to reflect reality. Here, as elsewhere, there is no simple answer.

Devising test types

Expediency will require that the tests be as practicable as possible (short, easily understood and easily administered and marked). But they must also be valid (test what they are supposed to test) and reliable (consistent in the assessment of different pupils). Given the backwash effect, they must be as close as possible to the language skills and activities which have been stated as objectives. Against this background of general factors, whose importance will vary according to the outlook of the group, a number of more specific issues have to be faced and settled.

CONTINUOUS ASSESSMENT AND SUMMATIVE ASSESSMENT

At their logical extremes, these two kinds of assessment are very different in nature, and have far-reaching effects on the teaching and testing situation. Most of the original graded language tests consisted of a summative test for each level, administered in a block; the main value of the tests, which were much simpler in form than the 16+ ordeals they were meant to replace, lay in the 'surrender value' of their language and skill content. Continuous assessment, which in modern languages as in other subjects has grown considerably in documentation and practice over the last few years, has several apparent advantages: it allows the detailed, short-term sampling of the syllabus; its extra coverage of the syllabus offers greater reliability; 'exam periods' are not necessary; it is often non-centralized, allowing greater teacher involvement in the devising of tests, and learner involvement in the filling-in of progress cards (which appear to be extremely popular and motivating); it offers a better diagnostic check for teacher and pupil. On the other hand, continuous assessment requires fairly sophisticated managerial skills on the part of the teacher. The use of very detailed checklists or progress cards may militate against interactive language, and continuous assessment is probably less suited to adult and further education.

Despite their dissimilarity, continuous and summative assessment may both be used in the same scheme; in fact, most forms of continuous assessment are reinforced by a periodic summative test, usually of a more global type than the regular detailed tests.

THE TESTER

In a continuous assessment scheme where learners equipped with materials such as progress cards test each other, the teacher's role may be simply that of the monitor who applies assessment criteria (see 'Scoring' below) to the speaking and listening skills of individual learners. In a summative test, listening is usually tested as a discrete skill, by means of multiple-choice or other objective answers, which are relatively easy to administer to a whole class. When spoken language has to be tested, it is again almost always the teacher who conducts the test on an individual basis. The familiarity of the pupil with the teacher will (usually) help create a more relaxed atmosphere for communication. Particularly at later levels, however, the argument for the test being conducted by an outsider (a visitor, another teacher, a native speaker, an outside examiner) appears stronger. First, there may be some doubt about the objectivity of an involved class teacher; the role of examiner may be considered too skilled to entrust to a class teacher (though with proper support for teachers, it should be possible to overcome these first two objections, as already happens in the case of many of the present oral examinations run by public examination boards). Perhaps more importantly, it may be considered that, as communication in the foreign language will eventually be carried out with a relatively unknown person, the test should go some way towards reflecting this reality. An overriding consideration in the question of who conducts the test will no doubt be the permanent availability of the teacher, whose services require no special payment. The commitment of the teacher, in terms of time, to the conducting of oral tests is a factor which needs to be recognized and adequately provided for by the planners of school timetables and examination routines.

NARRATIVE CONTEXT OR NOT?

Some groups have produced tests in which the listening and reading components are woven together into the form of story-line. The coherence this gives reflects reality more accurately, it is claimed, than a number of separate, disjointed items in each of the two skills. It also helps as an aid to memory, particularly for weaker learners. Individual groups will need to look carefully at both formats before deciding which reflects their objectives more closely – and which will prove easier to construct.

LISTENING TESTS

Where these are treated separately from speaking, the main considerations must be:

Pre-recording. The pre-recording of the test will standardize for all pupils the speed and clarity of delivery, and will make more accessible the voice of a native-speaker. More than one voice may be heard, and appropriate sound effects may be included. On the other hand, it may be difficult to arrange, and the recording will lack both the familiarity of the teacher's voice (so penalizing nervous candidates, especially at earlier levels), and the gestures and other paralinguistic features of 'naturalistic' communication (although it may be questioned how many teachers indulge in these anyway). It may be early days yet, but the advantages of video recording should also be borne in mind; most secondary schools already have at least one video recorder. Another form of input which has been proposed is a live, largely unscripted interview between native-speakers – an eminently realistic situation which may, however, be difficult to set up on any scale, and difficult to moderate at the levels for which objectivity will be an important consideration.

Content. The most appropriate types may be:

> announcements of the kind to be heard at railway stations, supermarkets or other public places;
> information such as 'guided tours', weather and traffic conditions from radio, television or 'ansafone' services;
> information given in reply to enquiries likely to be made in 'survival' situations;
> tapes from a twinned school; and
> overheard conversations in situations where relevant information will need to be understood, at least in outline (such as in a foreign home, or at a café with a group of friends).

The latter case should not be extended into a general 'fly-on-the-wall' prescription, in which any form of dialogue can be turned into a test; nor should any of the often-used types of 'Who is speaking?/Where are they?/What are they doing?' be adopted without first considering whether they are realistic or relevant.

Richness of language. If a defined syllabus is in existence, a conscious decision will need to be made as to whether listening tests should include only material from the syllabus, or the more 'realistic' mixture of syllabus and non-syllabus material.

Length. The above categories will provide a range of lengths of utterance, from the single simple sentence to the longer dialogue. Variety of length and of type should be aimed at within any test, although longer items may be easier than shorter ones, due to their extra contextual material.

Repetition. Although in normal circumstances most things will be heard once only, there is a strong case for repeating each utterance or dialogue heard in the test, on the grounds that repetition may normally be asked for in conversation, that official announcements are often repeated, and that extraneous noise or a slip in concentration should not be confused with lack of understanding.

Learner response. The degree of detail to be understood may vary from gist (What is this announcement about? Does it apply to me? Is she telling me off?) to specific (What time does it start? Where do I go for washing-up liquid?). Multiple-choice answers have long been popular, perhaps less so now; they require a certain amount of reading skill (certainly in the foreign language, but also in English); they are difficult and subjective to construct; they should ideally be pre-tested and evaluated; and they lack face validity, appearing artificial rather than communicative. Against this should be set the fact that they are extremely easy and objective to mark. If well constructed, they can provide valid evidence of comprehension. The main alternative (discounting open-ended questions in the foreign language, which are a truly mixed, difficult and probably inappropriate skill), consists of answering open-ended questions in English. The objection to these is that it may be difficult to convey to the pupil the exact degree of information required, and open-ended items are not easy to mark objectively. However, if the amount of time and effort required for writing effective multiple-choice questions is put into the composition of open-ended questions which are both explicit and objective, both these difficulties may be overcome.

There is another variety of possible response which involves the use of visuals, either by themselves or with written text. In the first kind, a spoken utterance gives specific information – the kind of shop being looked for, the position of a bank, the whereabouts of a friend – which has to be conveyed by the pupil's selection of one out of a number of visuals, or the marking of that information on an incomplete visual.

A further development of this involves the deliberate use of reading skills at the same time as listening: a spoken message has to be compared with a written text (an advert for a hotel, a menu, a town brochure), and the pupil notes down any differences or discrepancies. What will need to be considered in these last two types of test is whether they reflect a communicative reality (when might pupils do this?) and whether they can be constructed without straining resources. In the case of the second type, the question of whether the mixing of the skills is desirable, and the demands of interpretation (particularly for weaker pupils) will have to be set against the sense of novelty and excitement it will create.

SPEAKING TESTS

A major consideration will be how to cue the learner's response in each of the two main kinds of speaking activity: 'transactional', in which some outcome (buying, finding, arranging) has to be brought about; and 'conversational', in which information has to be exchanged, attitudes expressed and/or social relations developed.

In transactional activities the task to be accomplished is frequently given in English on a cue-card. The more specific the instruction is ('Buy a kilo of pears'), the easier the response is to mark objectively – but the closer it comes to an unrealistic piece of translation. The more the pupil has to interpret the instruction, however ('Find out whether they have any pears' = 'Est-ce que vous avez des poires?'), the greater the test of general intelligence, and the more subjective the marking. The use of visuals (representing, for example, goods to be bought) seems to work well at a simple level, where the information given often concerns a concrete object. At a more advanced level, however (such as showing blank conversation 'balloons' in a series of visuals), the question of difficulty of interpretation, and the marking of a *variety* of interpretations will need to be overcome by familiarization with the practice on the part of both learner and teacher. The tendency seems increasingly to be to set a global task which will allow the pupil a variety of ways of achieving the set aim ('Go into a shop and buy something for you and a friend to eat and drink on a picnic'). Not only is scope allowed here for improvisation and the suiting of personal tastes, but the shopkeeper/teacher can also be instructed as to what sorts of things are and are not available, thus requiring the pupil both to understand and to react accordingly. This, of course, involves the mixing of the oral and aural skills, due to a series of wholly natural constraints. Assessment of such an assignment will be relatively difficult but, given the use of criterion referencing (was it accomplished?) and criteria for assessing quality of language, far from impossible. The global form of task, as has been mentioned, also tests listening; this can also be done by asking the pupil to jot down the information s/he has gathered, such as the time of a train, the price of an article, a place to meet. (The complication then will be that the learner will have either to write whilst listening, or to remember the information for a while – and both of these activities could be unrealistic and inappropriate for most learners.) One solution may be to blend the different forms of cue, depending on the level of test and the type of situation.

Although 'transactional' is normally taken to be more or less synonomous with 'survival' language, it is a term which will extend beyond the usual shopping or way-finding into the kind of negotiating which may take place between friends, usually of the arrangement-making variety:

planning a night out, a holiday, or a day in town, based on information supplied in English or by foreign language realia. This is an activity which opens up exciting new possibilities, and seems particularly suited to the paired work useful for continuous assessment, where an outcome will be the natural consequence of the transaction. Whatever the form of the test, things to bear in mind are whether the different tasks set represent a reasonable sample of the syllabus; whether they are roughly equal between themselves; how many should be set; whether the less able should be presented with easier items or forms of item; and, if listening is tested, what weighting this should receive compared with speaking.

'Conversational' language, which is used to exchange information about a person's immediate environment and life-style, is likely to consist principally of a series of questions and answers. The most rudimentary form, which some groups have adopted for the early levels, is therefore that of a number of simple set questions (age, brothers and sisters, town, etc.). This rather uncommunicative format can be extended by naming the topic areas to be covered at each level, and leaving the teacher/tester to develop a series of appropriate questions and comments, including follow-up on information already given. This will still beg the question of how to prepare for this form of test – presumably by drilling a number of set questions, to which the answers will be learnt and 'parrotted' back. Here seems to lie the main difficulty in testing and teaching this kind of activity: however loosely framed the test is, and however interactive it may appear, the teaching and learning process is in danger of consisting largely of the learning of answers to a number of predictable questions. It may help to use outside native-speakers to conduct this part of the speaking test, and to ask for a certain amount of prepared exposition on a topic from each pupil (though here again the dangers of parrotting are obvious). Simulated situations in which the learner has to exchange information concerning such things as family, photographs, or question and give information to a supposed stranger in a train, all show potential for development, but whatever the alternative, there is a relative shortage of original thought or suggestion from the collected data on how to make this part of the test realistic, fair and interactive. It is an area in which research and development are obviously very necessary.

Another consideration needs to be borne in mind: the temptation will always be to require the learner to *answer* questions, whilst there should be a mechanism (either encouragement, or specific instructions on a cue-card), to bring about the *asking* of questions also; this will involve the need for the pupil to discriminate between the appropriate use of familiar and polite forms.

Finally, when it comes to the discussion of mixed or separate skills, it should be obvious that it will be virtually impossible, in a conversation, to separate listening and speaking, even at the simplest level of recognizing *which* of the prepared questions is being asked!

THE MECHANICS

A number of questions will still need to be settled about the administration of the tests, with the main emphasis again being on the speaking tests.

For the separate listening test, it will be helpful to keep it to a length which will fit comfortably inside a normal teaching unit. This will give a length of some 30 minutes, which should be ample at most levels.

For the speaking test, a number of details will have to be settled:

Place. The most convenient place to conduct the test is in the classroom. For this, quiet alternative activities will have to be found for the rest of the class; most schools seem to have been able to build up a bank of these. At higher levels, the question of security and leakage will occur, but it is generally felt that this will have a minimal effect on real communicative performance, especially when many of the assignments are already 'transparent'. Alternative locations for the test are in the corridor outside the classroom, or in a nearby cloakroom, both of which may require extra 'baby-sitting' facilities (although, more often than not, the rest of the class are trusted to get on quietly). The question of where the test takes place will be influenced by the relative importance for different teachers of practical convenience, on the one hand, and the dignity to be afforded the tests, on the other.

Timing. If not carried out during the lesson, as suggested above, the speaking test may take place at break, lunchtime or after school. Some teachers find this detracts from the prestige of modern languages, or is inconvenient, undignified or unnecessary; others consider it time well spent, if it means children are willing to give up their own time, if it means more room is available, and if it saves more time for learning.

The tape recorder. Without doubt, the recording of oral tests places an extra, if not intolerable strain on the tester as well as on the learner. If recording does take place, another person is sometimes used to operate the machine, although this may cause more problems (and shyness from the pupil) than it actually solves. The fact is, however, that a recording of at least some pupils will be essential for efficient moderating, whilst a more considered and fair marking will be possible in retrospect if all pupils are recorded. So another balance will have to be struck, between time and convenience, on the one hand, and reliability of marking on the other. Personal priorities will have influence here, as will the level of the test and the degree of reliability insisted upon. Cassettes, with counters, are generally considered quicker and easier to handle than open-reel tapes.

Prompting. For reliable tests, there must be a policy on prompting. The more specific the tasks that pupils have to accomplish (the more transparent their task), the less prompting is likely to be necessary. Possible attitudes range from the extremely strict (no prompting at all), through the repetition of a question, the re-phrasing of a question, the explanation of a written cue in English ('How do you say "No, thank you"?'), to the leaving of all prompting to the discretion of individual teachers. Prompting style must also be considered: is the tester to prompt like a teacher finding out what is known or like a sympathetic native-speaker, co-operating in getting the message across? It is no less important to stipulate *when* prompting should take place (after a certain length of time, in cases of embarrassment, in order to correct), and to what extent prompting will affect marks gained – if at all. It is apparent that such a number of delicate decisions cannot be left entirely to discretion – hence the crucial need for a policy. It is also clear, however, that a policy alone will not be sufficient, either. Conducting an oral test is without doubt one of the most skilled and sensitive tasks a language teacher may be called upon to perform. It is another area where in-service training is essential; so far it has been a case of training and experience being acquired *through* graded oral tests, rather than *for* them. It would not seem preposterous to suggest that the training agencies – advisers, LEAs, Department of Education and Science, university departments of education, colleges of education, and professional associations – could now take up some of the running.

Length. Expediency demands a streamlined test, the importance of spoken language demands a thorough one. The familiar paradox is normally resolved in a well-prepared test aiming to sample the whole (or most of the) syllabus, conducted rapidly, and spending between two and five minutes on each pupil (see Chapter IV). In this way, a class of 30 pupils could be examined (just) in two lessons of 35 minutes or, at most, in just over four lessons. Some teachers consider this expensive in time, hence the move towards testing outside normal teaching time. For the same reason, oral tests which require no interaction may be conducted in the language laboratory, and marked later. Experts in this technique have refined it to the point where the stimulus is read out, but not recorded, so that on playback, all that is heard is a connected string of responses, which can be quickly marked. Although this practice is not common, at levels where interaction is not required it appears to have considerable time-saving advantages.

Scoring

The question of when to assess speaking performance – live or on tape – has already been discussed above. The question of who should score it will be decided by the fact that, provided a suitable moderating process is built in (see below), the teacher is by far the most convenient, if not the best person available. Whether scoring takes place during a paired task, with the teacher monitoring, or during a summative test conducted by the teacher, there will be several factors to be borne in mind, increasing in scope and complexity with each succeeding level. In those cases where a graded test overlaps with a public examination, the practice will normally be for the teacher to assess initially, and for the results to be moderated, as for a CSE Mode III, working in groups or in a 'paired school' system. It is not yet clear whether those groups hoping to fit in with the GCE system will have to agree to external assessment, or whether initial school-based assessment will be retained.

One of the most important single questions raised by the graded objectives movement is the principle of criterion referencing, particularly in the assessment of spoken language. Whether it is a question of assessing a single-phrase utterance or a global task, the important principle will be: would that piece of language have achieved the communicative purpose for which it was intended? In order to decide whether the answer would be 'yes' or 'no', 'did' or 'didn't', the assessor is normally assumed to adopt the role of a sympathetic native speaker – a role simple enough in theory, but which may be difficult for a non-native under stress to achieve without practice. If the utterance is deemed successful, then a pass must be awarded, as the whole aim of communication has been achieved.

After this remains the question of *quality* of utterance: was it the bare minimum necessary, or did it have qualities which deserve further recognition? The assessor's role here is to decide to what degree, if any, these qualities have been exhibited; the job of the test developers is to establish what those qualities are, and how they should be expressed. So far this practice is in its infancy, but dimensions currently thought important include: accent, intonation, speed of delivery, length of utterance, range of vocabulary, grammatical accuracy, fluency, appropriateness, strategies for communication, amount of offence caused to native speaker's ear. Some or all of these parameters can be given a range of points (0–3, 0–5, 0–10), and the resulting total converted into a level of, say, four grades: fail, (bare) pass, credit, distinction. Detailed reference is made in Chapter IV, pp. 44–50. Although these dimensions have been used in a variety of forms and degrees of refinement by the public examination boards, their further elaboration is likely to be accelerated by the growth of graded tests. Transactional language is likely to be more straightforward to assess, as the line between success and failure to communicate will probably be clearer than in a conversation, where the task is less clear.

One point that has been made elsewhere (Chapter 4), but is worth repeating, is that, if 'communicative effectiveness' is accepted as a central criterion, it is quite possible to achieve a pass level in an utterance which contains errors of such things as gender, agreement, or verb ending. The implication of this is that the rigid attitude to error, particularly grammatical error, which has been customary for so many years will need to undergo a radical reappraisal on the part of teachers. Here is another case for in-service training.

Moderating

This has already been referred to under 'Scoring', to which it is closely related. In the case of discrete listening tests, little or no moderation will be necessary if the tests are designed with objective answers, as suggested. In the case of mixed-skill testing, either continuous or summative, certain procedures will lead to greater efficiency. Pre-recorded tests (either simulated or from previous years), played and discussed before the actual tests, will give teachers the confidence that will help them relax and make them more efficient examiners and assessors. After the tests have been conducted, a selection of candidates from each centre should be listened to and discussed by the group, and common standards set. For this, each centre need record only a few pupils, but the selection of a certain number from the whole range of candidates will make for greater reliability. The degree of insight and experience gained at moderating meetings is considered by many teachers to be one of the most formative influences on their careers; again, graded tests are seen to be a potent source of in-service training.

Grading

If the tasks set are realistic, according to the perceptions of teachers, then the majority of pupils will be expected to fulfil the majority of them. Most groups, as has already been noted, seem to expect about 90 per cent of pupils to achieve success, but the percentage of marks (or of instances of communication achieved) deemed necessary to qualify for 'success' varies more widely than might have been expected – from about 50 per cent (perhaps a dubious description of success) to over 70 per cent. The balance to be struck here is between describing criteria which will motivate the huge majority of pupils by putting them within their grasp, and offering sufficient challenge to maintain the involvement of able pupils. A major factor in the latter will be not just the degree of difficulty, but the relevance and inherent interest for all pupils of all the language activities they need to perform. Therefore test type, content and teaching methods will be more important considerations than simple statistics.

In addition to deciding a pass level for the individual skills or parts of the examination, groups will also have to establish whether each component will represent a 'hurdle' which every pupil will have to jump, or whether the final result will be based on aggregate alone. If a hurdle system is decided on (because, for example, it is felt the skill of speaking is important enough to necessitate a specified basic level of performance), it will be important to establish levels which still allow success for the majority.

Once basic pass levels are established, it must be decided whether additional levels of performance are to be recognized. The higher the pass mark, the less will be the spread of marks available for this distinction; given an average pass mark of 70 per cent, however, it should be quite easy to distinguish from the remaining spread of 30 per cent at least one level of extra performance.

Certificating

Apart from the question of which crest and whose signature should go on the certificate, two main issues will have to be decided: who certificates are for, and consequently, what type of language to use, and how detailed the description should be. Most groups seem to have avoided the trap of using jargon in their certificates – which seem to be aimed at pupils and parents and, possibly, employers – and concentrate on words such as 'coping', 'able to understand and express themselves', together with a list of the topics and situations covered at each level. Where a syllabus is expressed in functions, the problem of communicating with non-language teachers will be more difficult; one way out may be to describe these under the general term 'language activities' and list the topics covered – provided, of course, these also are specified in the syllabus.

The degree of detail shown is another question which will have to meet the constraint of being intelligible to the average pupil or parent. Usually, skills are specified either separately (listening, speaking and reading) or jointly (listening and speaking, reading and writing, 'talking'). If skills are considered to be too intermingled to be separated, then tasks can be mentioned instead (buying things, getting about, making arrangements), without reference to skills. The area of conversational topics is sometimes referred to as 'getting to know someone', followed by a list of the subjects covered (home, family, hobbies, school). The certificate may show simply that a pass has been achieved, or it may indicate a further degree of competence (see above). In addition, it may be considered desirable to show a level of performance on each skill, topic or activity, thus presenting a profile (Harrison, 1982, p. 39). The time and space required to produce and present this will have to be balanced against the possible value it may have for its recipients; the decision may not be an easy one!

A much wider question is whether the certificate will attempt to describe also the kinds of personal and intellectual qualities considered necessary to achieve success in the specified objectives. It may be argued that if aims other than purely linguistic are expressed or implied in the syllabus, then they should be shown on the certificate. Indeed, for some teachers, qualities such as perseverance, concentration, independence, ability to work alone and with others, understanding and appreciation of the foreign way of life, may be at least as important as the manipulation of language – even allowing for the fact that the former are not necessarily separable from the latter.

Evaluating

The first flush of success which the graded tests have achieved should not hide the fact that, in retrospect, many of them appear relatively crude. Some of the groups who were early in the field have realized increasingly the lack of sophistication of their early tests, particularly in listening and speaking, and are busy revising syllabuses and tests. More recent groups, however, appear to be well aware of the pitfalls and subtleties, and are developing tests of considerable sophistication. Evaluation is often low on the list of priorities, but as well as the thorough and objective type exemplified in Chapter IV, there is a more informal process of revision which is more practicable and therefore, at the moment, more common: the constant looking back and discussion of syllabus, tests and pupil performance, and checking to what extent they still reflect the developing aims of the group. As in-service work, this is extremely valuable; as a means of test development it is haphazard and slow. Formal evaluation projects are not unknown (considerable work has been done by OMLAC, the East Midlands Regional Examination Board (EMREB), and Cumbria/Lancashire), but they are rare enough to suggest that more resources will be required in this area both in order to maintain momentum, and to meet the challenge of public examinations.

Feeding back

Graded tests were seen initially as a carrot for pupils, especially for weaker pupils, and a catalyst for better teaching practice. The undoubted success of the tests, at least in terms of motivation, and their steady improvement, have not necessarily been matched, however, by any increase in communicative practice in the classroom. At a basic level, it is possible to conceive of the tests being 'taught' or superimposed on an existing syllabus or teaching methodology, and then forgotten until the following year. This extreme situation will be rare; it will be much more common for the influence of the tests to be felt in an increasing adaptation of teaching styles to match the communicative aims of the tests. But, although much has been learnt about the use of communicative tests, the actual input required to help pupils towards proficiency is still a relatively undocumented area. The dangers of learning lists – whether they be words, phrases, functions or even 'global communication strategies' – are well known, but there appears to be a dearth of real alternatives at the initial teaching stage. The creation of 'information gaps' is an excellent strategy for *practice*, but we need to know more about strategies for input, by means of research into methodology of the kind carried out by GLAFLL and EMREB.

There will be no overnight transformation of teaching practice, but rather a sifting of present practices, the retention and improvement of those which fit in with expressed aims, and the gradual elimination or adaptation of those which do not. The results of this operation may not be very predictable: there may well still be lists of vocabulary and other chunks of language to be learnt by rote; and a grammatical structure to language will have to be made increasingly explicit and learnt. Writing, although not always tested, may be given a more realistic function in the sequence of learning; and some of the tenets of the relatively recent audio-visual revolution may have to be abandoned.

The individual outcomes of this reappraisal will be unpredictable and, like any old wine in new bottles, not immediately recognizable. One overall effect which may be more evident, however, is a new atmosphere in a classroom in which communication is the main aim. It has also been suggested elsewhere that needs analysis is best carried out in conjunction with pupils. This collaboration and involvement will be reinforced by progress cards and continuous assessment, by the cooperation pupils need to provide in the actual administration of tests, and by pupils' increased awareness of their own goals and eventual achievement. In short, learning may eventually become pupil-centred rather than teacher-centred, with all the beneficial educational and professional outcomes this will entail.

Problems to be avoided will be the over-provision of materials for independent learning, such as worksheets, more pair and group work than pupils can realistically be expected to handle, and the confusion of precise, short-term language training objectives with overall educational aims. The sharing of experience between teachers and the spirit of enquiry with which exercises in communication have to be carried out should, however, greatly help to avoid major errors of judgement.

VI.   Other subject areas

It would be pretentious to claim that this report, with its limited scope and resources, could provide firm and precise guidelines for the application of graded tests to other subject areas, whose content must be as diverse as it is unfamiliar to most foreign language specialists. All that can be hoped is that some general pointers, based on the information contained in this report and the findings of Andrew Harrison (1982, pp. 46–51), will help with the initial orientation of other interested colleagues.

Relative importance of oral/aural skills

It could be suggested that in few other subject areas will the oral/aural component be as great as in a modern language learnt for the main purpose of communication. Although many subjects in Britain have a strong bias towards written language, this was not always so; and in many European countries, at least, the simple idea of an individual or group viva, assessed by an individual or a panel, is of long standing and is not considered unsuitable even for subjects dealing largely in concepts. We may also have a good deal to learn from cultures (in the Middle East, for example), where the spoken word has always had greater prominence than in our own. In the end, the oral/aural component possible in testing other subjects, particularly English, may be greater than is often realized.

Motivation

The growth of the graded objectives movement has been accelerated by the intense feeling of dissatisfaction felt by many teachers over the image presented by modern languages in the schools, of a selective elitist and somewhat archaic subject leading to a limited range of depressingly inappropriate examinations, and which a large number of pupils choose to abandon. It is to be hoped that despair is not a necessary basis for curriculum development, but it is obvious from the GOML movement that the will and the ability to re-examine and restructure a scheme of learning and examining must come from within, from the teachers themselves; a degree of frustration will leaven the workings of any group meeting to pool experience and expertise. Graded tests should aim, therefore, to tackle the weakest points on any subject curriculum.

Setting goals

The importance of the need to restructure tests and syllabuses, based on a radical reassessment of the needs or terminal objectives of a subject (or each stage of a subject) has been stated often enough here. The need is also reflected in the current attempt to establish national criteria for a common system of examining at 16+. The experience of the graded objectives movement suggests the following guidelines:

analysis of the kind of skills or achievements most likely to be needed by the learner at the end of a particular stage, bearing in mind the level of achievement attainable by the majority of learners, and the possible trade-in value of the certification involved;

the setting-out of these objectives in easily comprehensible, individual tasks;

the devising of testing techniques and settings which will recreate as accurately as possible a real-life speaking and listening situation;

the working-out of a consensus on the criteria to be applied to the assessment of utterances or responses other than those of a straight yes/no or multiple-choice kind (if these are to be included);

the setting of standards attainable by the majority of well-taught learners;

the choice of the wording and kind of definition to be shown on the certification, to describe accurately and clearly the achievement it represents;

the consideration of the ultimate effect of these tests on classroom teaching; and

whether they will translate into good classroom practice and materials.

Assessment of the spoken word

Of the activities in the previous paragraph, the one where most experience has been gained by the graded test movement (as revealed in this book), is in the assessment of the spoken word. Information will be found in sections on pp. 35–6 and 68–9 which may well be applicable to other subject areas – in particular, the idea of effective communication as a basic criterion (with its consequent reconsideration of the importance of accuracy and error), and the working-out of a number of scales (pronunciation, grammatical accuracy, fluency) against which a finer assessment can be made.

Support systems

Graded tests are not to be entered into lightly. They should not be embarked upon unless a school or group is sure it has, or can realistically hope for, a wide range of resources: committed teachers; willing leaders able to be 'boffin' and/or administrator; premises; transport; duplicating and secretarial facilities; the ability to arrange and participate in meetings, workshops and conferences of the kind organized by the GOML Co-ordinating Committee; and, unless the foregoing are liberally provided, a certain amount of finance. The commitment of all these resources, and the necessary adaptation of the normal school timetable, are amply justified by the benefits of adequate and thorough oral/aural tests.

Familiarization

The vanguard of the graded test movement in foreign languages has made impressive progress. Many teachers, even within the movement, must feel overwhelmed by the content and degree of the documentation produced, especially as they grapple with the reality of the working of the tests and their other everyday chores. The need for in-service training to help keep teachers abreast with developments, has already been mentioned, at the same time as the enormous contribution that the tests themselves have already made to in-service training by involving teachers in an exciting and stimulating new venture. The realization of the need for a regularized INSET network and of the great potential that graded tests can offer to it, will be essential to any other subject areas hoping to embark on a similar operation.

Cooperation

One of the hallmarks of a successful graded test group is the ability of its members to work together, often in an intense atmosphere and pooling individual skills. This internal cohesion is the basis for developing a clear decisive attitude towards outside bodies such as examination boards.

Information gathering

Although not directly related to the findings of the report, one discovery we made in the course of our investigations was the usefulness of gathering information by oral/aural techniques, instead of by written text. The method of recorded interview, in which an informant could be 'primed' before and between recordings, using the pause button, was fast, convenient and productive. It was also a vindication of our belief in the importance of oral/aural skills.

VII. The next step

During the course of planning this report, the subcommittee was aware of the large amount of documentation which needs to be obtained and studied to get a clear idea of the background to and latest developments in graded tests. The sources mentioned in the Bibliography and the work of the GOML committee play an important part in this; but the dynamic nature of the GOML groups means that new developments constantly need tracing and putting into perspective. This chapter is an attempt to identify areas which our investigations suggest would benefit from further explanation and investigation.

Assessing needs

A claim has already been made for the primary role of needs analysis in working towards an ideal definition of the testing and teaching situation for a group or several groups of learners (see Chapter V, 'Finding the right language'). The point has also been made that this implies a learner-centred, as opposed to a teacher-centred or language-centred, approach. If this is accepted, then the question must be asked: just how learner-centred is the analysis? How much do we know, and how have we come to know it, about the real needs of the learner? And who is the learner – is it a term which includes adults in further education centres, as has been claimed? If so, surely their needs will be very different from those of a 16-year-old. Having been radical about so many aspects of the learning situation, have we really re-thought sufficiently the practical and psychological needs of the learners? If Level 1 is taken largely by 12-year-olds, and Level 4 by 16-year-olds, do we offer what they are likely to need at each of those very different stages of development, or aim at some theoretical endpoint?

Some groups have responded to this challenge by basing the different levels on increasingly independent trips to the foreign country (from day trip to family stay). Others appear simply to have inherited a list of topics and situations from extant examination syllabuses, or from Council of Europe publications aimed initially at adults, adapted according to criteria which one suspects were not based on pupil-centred research. The point is not that any of these approaches are wrong for the learners for whom they were designed, or for any learner, but that we appear to have very little evidence on what pupils do actually need to say in a foreign language. To take one simple example: how much shopping is actually done in shops other than supermarkets, and what is the relative importance in a shopping situation of speaking ('I would like', 'There you are'); or of reading (labels, posters, shop signs); or of listening (availability, price); or of non-linguistic features (pointing, sign language, influencing people by looking friendly)? Is it unrealistic to suggest that teachers (and syllabus-designers) are too far away from the plight of a beginner to be able to recall the agony and the excitement, and that a superimposition of a succession of language-learning theories fetters the imagination?

Possibly the very different approaches to language testing (and teaching) shown by the groups are absolutely right (and the teaching situation and target populations differ enormously); or else it doesn't matter in the long run *what* you teach, within certain limits. Or there is room for further exploration of target group requirements. If such research is necessary, it is a first step, and not an eventual refinement.

Syllabus design

The variety of types of syllabus design to be found in the different groups were pointed out on p. 28. This is no doubt a source of strength, but the lack of a common approach might prove an obstacle to development. Some groups work from a simple list of situations and topics, assuming that teachers will know, or find out, the language input necessary to deal with them. Other groups list notions and functions as well as (or instead of) topics and situations, with or without language exponents for each function (in some cases, micro-function). Yet others are explicit about the kind of structure and/or vocabulary necessary to cope with each situation or function, or with the syllabus as a whole; many adopt an eclectic approach.

The question behind this variety of approach appears to be: how predictable is language, and to what extent can it be defined and described? This follows on directly from the question of needs analysis mentioned above. Another important question is: does definition help or hinder the production of language? There may well be no final solution to the questions, but the relatively primitive state of the art, or at least the gulf between theory and practice, points again to the need for further research, contrastive analysis and the pooling of ideas.

Evaluation

The analysis in Chapter IV of specific oral/aural tests is a small-scale example of the kind of detailed examination which needs to be carried out in order to evaluate the tests, particularly in relation to their syllabus: to see whether, for example, skills listed discretely are tested discretely; whether a notional syllabus is tested purely through situations; whether specified vocabulary is used exclusively; whether the syllabus is adequately sampled in the whole test or in individual skills, and whether alternative forms of the same test (such as role-play assignments) are equal in length and difficulty. An extension of this form of detailed evaluation would help ensure the validity and respectability of the tests, particularly when they come to be compared with public examinations, whose banks of data are unlikely to include information of this kind.

The role of reality

One complaint often made by members of the graded test movement against GCE and CSE language examinations is the artificiality of some of the skills required, such as telling a story in pictures, reading aloud and answering set questions. As a consequence, there is an attempt to introduce realistic tasks in some of the graded tests, and there is still obviously a lot of work to be done in developing and extending this principle into a wider range of practical assignments. This is a long-term and complex task, but there are three possible objections to its usefulness: first, the testing situation, by its very nature, can never be 'real' – it will always be a test, and will always demand a degree of simulation, so attempts to make it absolutely real are doomed to failure. Second, there is a strong possibility that the requirements of objectivity militate against reality; a truly free, open-ended multi-skill interactive test will be very difficult to assess reliably, whilst the truly objective test exemplified by multiple-choice answers is as much a mockery of reality as is telling a story in pictures. Third, test forms embodying new ideas soon atrophy into 'exam questions', making constant revision necessary.

Again, the main conclusion to this observation is the extent of our unsureness about the relative merits of reality and objectivity, and about the other factors involved such as the backwash effect on teaching, and the need to find out as much as we can about them.

Teaching a syllabus

Another criticism which is often levelled at the examination boards is the fact that their modern language syllabuses are scanty or non-existent, and that, as a result, examination content can only be surmised from a study of old papers, which come to constitute a very imperfect syllabus. As has already been pointed out, the graded test syllabuses are very different from each other, so generalization is difficult, but it is not certain that they all provide a perfectly adequate teaching base. A syllabus expressed in terms of topics and situations may lend itself quite easily to situational classroom practice, but unless, for example, the range of 'drinks' envisaged – and tested – in the task of 'order drinks from a café' is specified, or some idea is stated of the kind of 'information about one's family' which will need to be given, the teacher may easily make a number of wrong suppositions. Here the collaboration and sharing of information which comes from a close-knit group will be vital, but without more clearly defined exponents there is a danger that past papers will again come to form the syllabus.

... the objectives have been described in *output syllabuses*, i.e. they state what a pupil is expected to be able to *produce* at a given stage of learning, given the possibility of presenting his knowledge according to his own rate of progress. This is all very well, but the weakness of an output syllabus is that it does not tell us *how the pupil can achieve* the specified communicative competence. This will require comprehensive practical development of methods, mainly by individual teachers and by teaching teams ... (Bergentoft, 1980, our emphasis)

In the case of syllabuses which are expressed in terms of functions and notions, with a list of exponents, it cannot be immediately clear to teachers how to go about teaching these. Functions and notions are as much the 'bits and pieces' of language as is grammar, and it will be important to bear in mind that:

nor does the learning of lists of functions and notions lead directly to an ability to complete such tasks [authentic communicative tasks]. (C R I)

We need to know much more about the kind of teaching activity which leads to successful completion of the different levels of the graded tests, and about the ways in which syllabus description can be most helpful to teachers of a wide range of styles in preparing pupils for the tests.

... the visitors had the impression that language teaching did not incorporate a concerted approach to methods. Teaching was ... sometimes conducted on very traditional lines, often with functional elements included, but very seldom with a communicative approach in the true sense of the term ... (Bergentoft, 1980)

Assessment

Assessment is a difficult subject to consider entirely on its own; it is closely related to the criteria on which the tests are based, and therefore to the content and style of the learning/teaching process. This interrelationship is intensified in the case of self- and continuous assessment, where testing and teaching can become almost inseparable parts of the same process. What is certain, however, is that information on the relatively new phenomenon of continuous assessment is essential, together with an analysis of its effect on and implications for classroom organization, teaching techniques, materials, and motivation. Above all, we must bear in mind the profound impact it is likely to have on the teacher-pupil relationship. Individualized learning is still not a very common feature, but there is no doubt that the development of the assessment of communication in pairs or groups points towards individualization, self-awareness and, eventually, democratization within the classroom.

A more specific consideration concerning assessment is the degree of skill required by the assessor in defining and applying criteria to pupil utterances, no matter how long these utterances are. Various guidelines are available as to the kind of 'grid' which can be used (see pp. 68–9), and no doubt these can be adapted to fit specific circumstances and particular theories. Clearly, more research is needed into the reliability and validity of the proposed criteria. A further step is to make teachers aware of, and expert in, the use of these grids, particularly in a live test situation. There is a suggestion that teachers are able, with practice, to separate the role of sympathetic foreigner and unbiased marker. This is encouraging, although again much more research is necessary. The plethora of tests administered each year must have built up an enormous body of expertise, and the question now must be how to provide the resources and machinery to make that expertise more readily available.

Criterion referencing has also received some exposure in this report, albeit usually in the form of questions rather than answers. Any conclusions which can be reached on its applicability and relevance will form an important contribution to the development of oral/aural tests.

Definition of levels

Andrew Harrison has already clearly explained the possible ways of showing progression in the different levels of test (1982, p. 22): by expanding the situation, expanding the number of exponents for given functions, or increasing the functions. The commissioned reports suggest this may not be such an easy procedure; if pupils have already proved themselves competent in a particular task, how can they be asked to perform it at succeeding levels? Perhaps one solution to this problem is to take a broad area of communication (such as 'obtaining goods and services') and to treat it like an onion, peeling off a succession of layers of language necessary to perform it with increasing proficiency. This will require a precise description of what each layer consists of, in terms of tasks and language required to perform them. This question may well be complicated by the fact that the older learners are, the less inclined they appear to be to communicate:

Teachers have for years noted that younger pupils talk in the foreign language more readily than those in their mid-teens. Has this to do with maturation, going through a 'difficult stage', or is it related to course content, teaching techniques or other factors such as gender? (C R I)

Trade-in value

One of the most obvious virtues of a test which aims to develop the skill of communication by simulating listening and speaking situations as close as possible to those in real life, is that proficiency in these skills should lead to an ability to communicate in a foreign country or with a visiting foreigner – both as a tourist and as part of a job. Traditionally, G C E and C S E certificates have provided a quantitative measure as a qualification for jobs or further education. It would be wasteful and unrealistic if the potential of graded tests for developing life skills, and for giving an accurate profile of proficiency in a wide range of micro-skills, were to be neglected in favour of a simple pass/fail concept, to be added to a number of other pieces of paper. There is a clear need for further experimentation with economical yet informative ways of reporting on the learner's communicative proficiency. Also worth considering is building into the certification a number of other features – effort, tenacity, co-operation – which might be developed and assessed in a language course. A useful input required here would be from would-be employers, to find out what use, if any, they would make of graded test certificates.

Plotting the course

If the list of things we need to know about oral/aural tests seems unnecessarily long, it must be set against the even longer list of things dis-
covered and positive achievements made in the short history of graded
tests. The impressive bow wave of the movement should not hide the fact,
however, that the wake caused by such progress will not be smooth or
clear. The kind of guidance required by the uninitiated will be helped
by investigation of the points raised in this chapter and by a study of
what constitutes a good group. It is not a question of finding out which
GT model gives most cc – that will depend on individual circumstances –
but of finding out how the different models work and seeing what they
offer.

Appendix A   Titles and sources of commissioned reports*

CR I   'The problems of oral/aural assessment in schools: how they arise
            and how we try to solve them', Judith Hamilton, Research Officer,
            Graded Levels of Achievement in Foreign Language Learning
            (Lothian)†

CR II   'The administrative problems involved in setting graded tests (meet-
            ings, marking and moderation) and ways of solving them', David
            Peacock, Director, Institute of European Education, Lancaster
            (Cumbria/Lancashire)

CR III   'The assessing of oral responses: discrete marking, global assess-
            ments or other methods; the question of prompting', Norman White,
            Modern Languages Adviser (Hillingdon)

CR IV   'The separation of the speaking and listening skills: is it possible,
            and if so is it desirable?' David Cross (Archbishop Michael Ramsay
            School, ILEA)

CR V   'Continuous assessment, pair assessment and self-assessment: ad-
            vantages and practical considerations', Bernadette McGhee and
            Maggie Brady, Bushloe High School (East Midlands Regional Ex-
            amination Board Feasibility Study)

CR VI   'Non-verbal stimuli in the speaking test: their desirability, results
            so far and drawbacks', Ken Hall, Boston Spa Comprehensive School
            (Leeds)

CR VII   'The production of materials for the oral/aural tests: problems and
            solutions', Sheila Whiteside, Mark Hall Comprehensive School
            (Harlow/West Essex)

CR VIII   'Testing listening skills, considerations and problems: teacher or tape
            recorder, dialogue or narrative, length of item, content', Keith

* Available for reference purposes in the GOML 'green files' at CILT. See Bibliography.
† The names in brackets show the local GOML groups.

Gordon, Curriculum Development Leader, Witney Teachers' Centre (Oxford Modern Language Achievement Certificate)

CR IX   'The problems of oral/aural assessment in schools: how they arise, and how we try to solve them', Michael Gorman, Wolverhampton Polytechnic (Wolverhampton)

Appendix B Glossary

Affective	To do with attitudes or emotions, as opposed to facts.
Assessment	Testing.
Continuous assessment	Testing at short, regular intervals (cf. 'summative').
Self-assessment	Assessment by the pupil of his/her own ability to perform certain language tasks, usually recorded on a checklist or progress card.
Assignment	A job which has to be performed using language, such as buying food for a picnic, arranging a day out.
Communication	The exchange of language (spoken or written) for a specific purpose, of importance to the participants.
Communicative	Involving communication.
competence	Ability to communicate.
event	Effective exchange of language.
grammar	Grammar concerned with communication, as opposed to formal structure.
performance	Specific indication of the ability to communicate.
strategy	Any language device (request for repetition, polite formula, etc.) which helps to maintain communication.
syllabus	Syllabus expressed in terms of what needs to be communicated (and/or ways of doing so).
Criterion referencing	The assessment of performance against a specified criterion or level, as opposed to against other pupils (cf. 'norm referencing').
Diagnostic test	A test aimed at establishing the effectiveness or otherwise of initial teaching/learning and the need, if any, for remedial work.

Discrete	Separate, independent, as in 'discrete skill', 'discrete point' (cf. 'global', 'integrative').
Exponent	Language item (word, phrase, structure) suitable for the expression of a particular language function or notion (see below).
Function	A purpose to which language can be put, such as agreeing, disagreeing and persuading.
Functional	Expressed in terms of functions, as in 'functional syllabus'.
Global	Involving several dimensions of language performance, as in 'global assessment', which takes in several utterances or several features of one utterance.
Information gap	A situation in which one person has information which another has not, and in which that information has to be transferred from one to the other.
Information transfer	The conveying of information, as in the situation above.
INSET	In-service education and training.
Integrative	Involving several combined elements, as in 'integrative tests' which test more than one skill.
Interactive	In which people act upon each other with language, usually affecting each other's own language and behaviour.
Lexical	To do with words, as in 'lexical item' (= word).
Lock-step	All together, as dictated by average rate of progress or teacher control, as opposed to individual ability.
Needs analysis	The detailed study of the (language) needs of a specific individual or group in a specific situation.
Norm referencing	The assessment of performance of individuals against the performance of a group. (cf. 'criterion referencing').
Notion	A concept or idea which can be expressed by language, such as dimension, colour, result, frequency, time.

Notional	Expressed in terms of notions, as in 'notional syllabus'.
Phatic language	Language used to establish relations rather than convey meaning, as in 'How do you do?'.
Pragmatic	Practical, involved with getting things done, as in 'pragmatic language'.
Reliability	Accuracy and consistency in assessing.
Structural	Grammatical, concerned with the formal structure of language.
Summative	Coming at the end of a period of time, and assessing pupils' end performance on a block of items or information (cf. 'continuous assessment' and 'diagnostic test').
Task	Job which has to be carried out by the use of language (cf. 'assignment').
Transactional	In which a transaction has to take place, such as finding the way, getting medical treatment. Usually found in 'transactional language'.
Validity	The extent to which assessment reflects its aims as expressed, for example, in a syllabus.

Bibliography

Whilst many books and reports have been consulted during the course of this research project it was thought best to refer only to a small selection of those found most useful which might help colleagues immediately concerned with this work.

BERGENTOFT, R., 1980, *Intensive Visit Organised by the British Authorities Within the Framework of the Interaction Network in the School Sector of the Modern Languages Project* (document CC-GP4(80)16), Council of Europe, Strasbourg.

Exactly what the title says it is. A very perceptive report, giving penetrating and constructive criticism of some of the major early GOML projects, reporting on early progress and suggesting lines for further developments.

BROWN, S., 1980, *What Do They Know? A Review of Criterion-Referenced Assessment*, HMSO, Edinburgh.

A clear, thorough review of the whole area of criterion referencing, dealing with its technicalities, whether or not it is really possible, what the difficulties are, and demonstrating by means of a lengthy bibliography how much work has already been done and how much there is still to do.

BUCKBY, M., BULL, P., FLETCHER, R., GREEN, P., PAGE, B. and ROGER, D., 1981, *Graded Objectives and Tests for Modern Languages: an Evaluation*, Schools Council; available from CILT, 20 Carlton House Terrace, London SW1Y 5AP. Essential reading for anyone who wants to look at the only evaluation done so far of the effects of GOML work on motivation. Positive conclusions are reached.

CARROLL, B. J., 1980, *Testing Communicative Performance*, Pergamon, Oxford.

How to introduce more parameters than just 'right' or 'wrong' into assessment. Carroll makes definite proposals and this book has been a seminal text for several GOML projects.

COSTE, D., COURTILLON, J., FERENCZI, V., MARTINS-BALTAR, M., PAPO, E. and ROULET, E., 1976, *Un Niveau Seuil*, Council of Europe, Strasbourg.

The reference book for many GOML groups and staffrooms where real attempts are being made to devise syllabuses based on learners' perceived and expressed needs. It provides long checklists of items and deserves a place in every French department's book collection.

GOML Newsletter, CILT, published twice yearly. Price 50p. plus 20p. postage, but distributed free of charge to GOML groups, examination boards and modern language advisers.

HARDING, A., PAGE, B., and ROWELL, S., 1980, *Graded Objectives in Modern Languages*, CILT.
The basic GOML book, written by GOML for GOML and to let everyone else know what GOML was all about. This one gives all the contact addresses and details of schemes in 1980, with levels and future plans. See also below under 'Last but not least . . .'.

HARRISON, A., 1982, *Review of Graded Tests*, Schools Council Examinations Bulletin 41, Methuen Educational.
A review of the GOML movement commissioned by the Schools Council, this is a fair picture of the GOML scene in 1982 and the developments in the by now maturing projects, describing their impact on the wider educational scene and the world of examinations. Has a useful bibliography.

LITTLEWOOD, W., 1981, *Communicative Language Teaching: an Introduction*, Cambridge University Press.
The book the GOML Conference used in 1982 to help with the work in progress. Has a useful bibliography.

SATTERLY, D., 1981, *Assessment in Schools*, Theory and Practice in Education series, Basil Blackwell.
A very clear, detailed and comprehensive introduction to the whole area of assessment, ranging from a consideration of the underlying philosophy to detailed descriptions of how to set specific tests in schools and interpret the results.

Useful examples

Other useful examples of pioneering testing work are:

ARELS Examinations Trust, 1978, *ARELS Oral Examinations: Rationale, Development and Methods*, available from ARELS, 113 Banbury Road, Oxford OX2 6JX. (Revised edition due late 1983.)

ROYAL SOCIETY OF ARTS EXAMINATIONS BOARD, 1980, *Examinations in the Communicative Use of English as a Foreign Language: Specifications and Specimen Papers*.

ROYAL SOCIETY OF ARTS EXAMINATIONS BOARD, 1980, *Modern Languages: Preliminary Level Examination Explanatory Booklet*.

Last but not least . . .

The 'green files'. CILT holds details of all extant GOML projects in a set of green files which can be freely consulted at CILT. We found these useful for letting us know which projects we wanted to contact for further information. CILT: 20 Carlton House Terrace, London SW1Y 5AP.

Members of the monitoring and review group

A. H. Jennings (*Chair*)	Formerly Headmaster, Ecclesfield School, Sheffield; acting Chairman, Schools Council (Secondary Heads Association)
R. Aitken	Director of Education, Coventry (Association of Metropolitan Authorities)
B. C. Arthur	HM Inspectorate of Schools
J. J. Billington	Deputy Headmaster, High Pavement Sixth Form College, Nottingham (Assistant Masters and Mistresses Association)
D. Foster (*to December 1981*)	Headmaster, Churchill School, Bristol (CSE Examining Boards)
W. S. Frearson (*from March 1982*)	Ashford College, Middlesex (CSE Examining Boards)
J. C. Hedger	Department of Education and Science
P. M. Herbert	The Elliott School, London SW15 (National Association of Schoolmasters/Union of Women Teachers)
H. F. King (*from April 1982*)	Secretary, Oxford and Cambridge Schools Examination Board (GCE Examining Boards)
D. I. Morgan	Vice-principal, W. R. Tuson College, Preston, Lancs (National Union of Teachers)
R. Potts	Harraby Comprehensive School, Carlisle (National Union of Teachers)
A. R. Stephenson (*to March 1982*)	Secretary, University of London School Examinations Department (GCE Examining Boards)

Schools Council staff
G. Bardell · Assessment and Examinations Unit